Grammar Sense 1

WORKBOOK

Tay Lesley

OXFORD

UNIVERSITY PRESS

OXFORD
UNIVERSITY PRESS

198 Madison Avenue
New York, NY 10016 USA

Great Clarendon Street, Oxford OX2 6DP UK

Oxford University Press is a department of the University of Oxford.
It furthers the University's objective of excellence in research, scholarship,
and education by publishing worldwide in

Oxford   New York

Auckland   Cape Town   Dar es Salaam   Hong Kong   Karachi
Kuala Lumpur   Madrid   Melbourne   Mexico City   Nairobi
New Delhi   Shanghai   Taipei   Toronto

With offices in

Argentina   Austria   Brazil   Chile   Czech Republic   France   Greece
Guatemala   Hungary   Italy   Japan   Poland   Portugal   Singapore
South Korea   Switzerland   Thailand   Turkey   Ukraine   Vietnam

Editorial Manager: Janet Aitchison
Editor: Pietro Alongi
Associate Editor: Daria Ruzicka
Project Management and Production: Marblehead House, Inc.
Production Manager: Shanta Persaud
Production Controller: Zainaltu Jawat Ali

Illustrations: Roger Penwill, John Edens
Cover Design: LeeAnne Dollison
Cover Photo: Kevin Schafer / Peter Arnold, Inc.

ACKNOWLEDGEMENTS

*The authors and publisher are grateful for permission to reprint the following
photographs:* **p. 1**: ©Paul Barton/Corbis; **p. 50**: ©Michael S. Yamashita/Corbis;
p. 53: ©PhotoDisc; **p. 91**: ©PhotoDisc; **p. 109**: ©Richard T. Nowitz/Corbis.

ISBN: 978 0 19 436618 2

Printed in Hong Kong

10 9 8 7 6

Contents

1 Simple Present Statements with *Be*

FORM

1 Examining Form

Read about the people in the photos and complete the tasks below.

Alan Gold <u>is</u> the president of NewAge Communications. He <u>is</u> thirty years old. NewAge Communications <u>is</u> an Internet
5 service company in Boston. The company (isn't) very large, but (it's) successful.

John Porter and Luisa Diaz <u>are</u> new employees at NewAge
10 Communications. John and Luisa <u>are</u> in the sales department. They (aren't) in the office today. (They're) in a sales meeting.

My name <u>is</u> Lynne Wu. (I'm) in
15 the sales department at NewAge Communications, too. (It's) a great company. (I'm) the assistant to the sales manager. (I'm) at work this morning. (I'm) not in the sales
20 meeting.

1. Look at the underlined example of the affirmative simple present of *be*. Underline eleven more.

2. Look at the circled example of the negative simple present of *be*. Circle two more.

3. Find the contractions for *they are, I am, is not.* _____

2) Practicing Simple Present Statements with *Be*

Use the words and phrases to form sentences with the simple present of *be*. Punctuate your sentences correctly.

1. I / a computer technician

   <u>I am a computer technician.</u>

2. Computervilla / a new company

   <u>Computervilla is a new company.</u>

3. Bill / new employee

   <u>Bill is new employee</u>

4. We / not / students

   <u>We are not student</u>

5. Kelly / in a sales meeting

   <u>Kelly is in a sale meeting</u>

6. They / not / in the office

   <u>They are not in the office.</u>

3) Working on Pronouns and Contractions

Rewrite these sentences with pronouns and contractions.

1. Steve is smart.

   <u>He's smart.</u>

2. Julie Evans and Jack Lin are new employees.

   <u>They're new employee</u>

3. The company is not in Japan.

   <u>It's not in Japan</u>

4. The computers are new.

   <u>They're new</u>

5. Janice Howard is not the president.

   <u>She isn't the president.</u>

6. Jess and I are teachers.

   <u>We're teachers.</u>

7. You and Jack are at work.

   <u>You're at work.</u>

MEANING AND USE

4 Descriptions with *Be*

Use a word or phrase from the box to complete the sentences below.

at home	hot
a programmer	old ✓
from Brazil ✓	12 years old ✓

1. Anna is my sister. She's _12 years old_.

2. Greg isn't a doctor. He's _a programmer_.

3. We're young. We aren't _old_.

4. Luisa is not American. She's _from Brazil_.

5. Tom isn't at work today. He's _at home_.

6. It is August. It's _hot_.

5 Identifying Sentences with *Be*

Read the sentences below. What does each sentence talk about? Circle the correct answers.

1. Tom is a computer programmer.

   a. age   **b.** occupation

2. Umberto and Celia are from Honduras.

   a. origin   b. location

3. The boy is friendly.

   a. personality   b. physical characteristic

4. They're in the hospital.

   a. location   b. origin

5. Compugames is a large company.

   a. occupation   **b.** physical characteristic

6. I'm 27.

   a. origin   **b.** age

COMBINING FORM, MEANING, AND USE

6) Editing

Some of these sentences have errors. Find the errors and correct them.

1. I ~~isn't~~ *am not* tired.

2. Irina ~~be~~ *is* Russian.

3. He ~~not is~~ *isn't* in my class.

4. Peas and carrots are vegetables.

5. We're in school.

6. They ~~is~~ *are* from Japan.

7. You aren't old.

8. It ~~are~~ *is* hot and humid.

7) Writing

On a separate sheet of paper, write a paragraph about yourself. Use sentences with the correct form of *be*. In your paragraph, include this information:

- your name
- your age
- your country of origin
- your occupation
- your physical and personality characteristics

My name is Sam Lee. I'm 24 years old. I'm from

Taiwan . . . .

2 Questions with *Be*

FORM

1 Examining Form

Read the conversations and complete the tasks below.

CONVERSATION 1

Ana: How's your new roommate?

Ben: Paul? He's fine.

Ana: Is he nice?

Ben: Yes, he's very nice.

5 **Ana:** That's good. Is he a business major, too?

Ben: No, he's a music major.

Ana: Hmm. What's his favorite kind of music?

Ben: Classical, I think. I'm not sure.

CONVERSATION 2

Min-hee: Are you a new student?

10   **Jenny:** Yes, I am. My name is Jenny.

Min-hee: I'm Min-hee.

   Jenny: Where are you from? Are you from Japan?

Min-hee: No, I'm from Korea.

   Jenny: It's nice to meet you, Min-hee.

15 **Min-hee:** It's nice to meet you too, Jenny.

---

1. Look at the underlined example of an information question with *be*. Underline two more.

2. Look at the circled example of a *Yes/No* question with *be*. Circle three more.

Form simple present *Yes/No* questions. Use the correct form of *be* and the words and phrases below. Punctuate your sentences correctly.

1. you/doctor? _Are you a doctor?_____

2. Diego/from Mexico_____

3. I/late _____

4. you and Jack/students _____

5. we/ready _____

6. Veronica/busy _____

7. it/beautiful _____

8. they/lawyers _____

3 **Forming Information Questions with *Be***

Form information questions. Use the words and phrases below and the correct form of *be*.

1. who/you?
   A: _Who are you?_____
   B: I'm the new assistant.

2. where/your office?
   A: _____
   B: It's on Center Street.

3. when/the meeting?
   A: _____
   B: At three o'clock.

4. who/your friends?
   A: _____
   B: They're students in my class.

5. how/your boss?
   A: _____
   B: Fine.

6. what/on your desk?
   A: _____
   B: Some books.

7. where/we?
   A: _____
   B: On the third floor.

8. how/the weather?
   A: _____
   B: It's windy.

9. when/the wedding?
   A: _____
   B: August 1.

10. what/your name?
    A: _____
    B: Elena.

MEANING AND USE

4 **Matching Simple Present Questions and Answers with _Be_**

Match the questions on the left with the answers on the right.

_c_   **1.** Am I late?   **a.** Yes, it is.

____   **2.** When is class?   **b.** He's my roommate.

____   **3.** Where are your friends?   **c.** No, you aren't.

____   **4.** How is your sister?   **d.** 10 Garden Street.

____   **5.** Is Larry a mechanic?   **e.** They're at home.

____   **6.** Who is he?   **f.** It's in Spain.

____   **7.** Where is Madrid?   **g.** She's fine.

____   **8.** Is the house expensive?   **h.** They're not good.

____   **9.** What is your address?   **i.** No, he's not.

____   **10.** How are your grades?   **j.** At three o'clock.

5 **Writing Simple Present Information Questions with _Be_**

Read the letter to Julia. Then write information questions for the answers below.

1. A: How is Amy?

    B: She's great.

2. A: _____

    B: They're in Paris.

3. A: _____

    B: It's beautiful.

4. A: _____

    B: She's a new friend.

5. A: _____

    B: She's from Atlanta.

6. A: _____

    B: She's a teacher.

7. A: _____

    B: It's nice.

8. A: _____

    B: On Sunday.

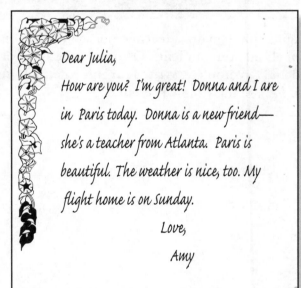

Dear Julia,

How are you? I'm great! Donna and I are in Paris today. Donna is a new friend— she's a teacher from Atlanta. Paris is beautiful. The weather is nice, too. My flight home is on Sunday.

            Love,

            Amy

COMBINING FORM, MEANING, AND USE

6 Editing

Some of the sentences in this conversation have errors. Find the errors and correct them.

Brad: Hi. Are you a student here?

Marcus: Yes, ~~I'm~~ ^{I am}. I'm a freshman.

Brad: What your name?

Marcus: My name Marcus.

Brad: I'm Brad. Where are from, Marcus?

Marcus: I from Beaver Falls.

Brad: That near here?

Marcus: No, it's a small town near Portland, Oregon.

Brad: What your major is?

Marcus: Chemistry.

Brad: Really? Chemistry it's my major, too!

7 Writing

Imagine that you are a teacher at a school. It is the first day of classes. You want to learn about your students. On a separate sheet of paper, write a questionnaire for the students to complete. Write four information questions and two *Yes/No* questions with *be.* Use the simple present.

What is your name?

Are you a new student?

3 Imperatives

FORM

1 Examining Form

Read the instructions and complete the tasks below.

Instructions:
<u>Stir</u> the paint well. Paint one coat and wait until dry. Finish with a second coat. Clean brush with
5 soap and warm water.

Directions to the Party:
• Take Route 130 south to Thorn Ave.
• (Don't take) the first exit at Thorn Ave.—take the second exit.
10 • Go west on Thorn Ave. to Arden Way and turn right . . .

WARNING: Do not eat. Do not swallow. Do not put in eyes. Keep away from children.

1. Look at the underlined example of an affirmative imperative. Underline nine more.

2. Look at the circled example of a negative imperative. Circle three more.

3. How is the negative imperative formed? _____

Complete the sentences below with affirmative or negative imperatives. Use the verbs below.

talk	close	forget	get	leave	turn	look	listen

1. <u>Don't forget</u> your appointment. It's today at 2:30.

2. _____ right. Don't go left.

3. Please be quiet. _____ during the test.

4. _____ out! A car!

5. Please _____ the door. It's cold.

6. _____. Stay here with me.

7. _____ to this new CD. It's great!

8. _____ me some coffee, please.

MEANING AND USE

3 **Working on Directions and Prepositions of Location**

Look at the map. Then complete the tasks below.

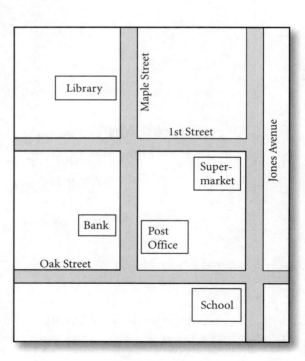

1. Give directions from the supermarket to the school.

    <u>Walk straight on Jones Avenue to Oak</u>
    <u>Street. The school is on the corner.</u>

2. Give directions from the library to the supermarket.

    _____

    _____

3. Give directions from the bank to the library.

    _____

    _____

4. Give directions from the post office to the school.

    _____

    _____

Understanding Meaning and Use

Match each sentence to the correct meaning and use.

_c_   **1.** Parent to child: "Get dressed!"

____   **2.** Label on bottle: "Do not drink!"

____   **3.** Man to tourist: "Go one block, then turn right."

____   **4.** In a cookbook: "Put the milk in a bowl."

____   **5.** Owner to pet: "Sit, Fido, sit!"

____   **6.** On a test: "Circle the correct answers."

a. instructions

b. warning

c. command

d. directions

COMBINING FORM, MEANING, AND USE

Thinking About Meaning and Use

Read each command and situation. Circle the appropriate situation for each command.

1. "Write these words in your notebook."
   a. police officer to a driver on a highway
   b. teacher to students in class

2. "Walk straight down this street."
   a. person to a stranger in a city
   b. man to a woman in a car

3. "Relax, and I will take your temperature."
   a. one student to another student in class
   b. doctor to a sick person in a hospital

4. "Don't be late for the meeting, please."
   a. parent to child at home
   b. boss to an employee in an office

5. "Go clean your room."
   a. mother to daughter
   b. student to teacher in class

6. "Take the elevator to the fourth floor. It's on the right."
   a. bus driver to a passenger
   b. salesperson to a customer in a department store

Read these class rules for new students. Some of the rules are incorrect. Change the incorrect affirmative sentences to negative sentences, and change the incorrect negative sentences to affirmative sentences.

1. ~~Don't be~~ *Be* quiet in class.

2. Study for your tests.

3. Eat in class.

4. Listen to the teacher.

5. Don't be on time for class.

6. Don't ask questions.

7. Leave your homework at home.

8. Don't be polite to the teacher.

7 **Writing**

On a separate sheet of paper, write one of the following:

• a set of instructions for making a simple recipe

• directions to a place near your school or your home

Include affirmative and negative imperatives in your list.

> *How to Make a Healthy Tuna Sandwich*
>
> 1. Open a can of tuna.
>
> 2. Put the tuna in a bowl.
>
> 3. Don't add mayonnaise.
>
> 4. Add two tablespoons of yogurt. . . .

Chapters 1–3

A. Complete the conversations with the simple present of *be*. Use contractions where possible.

1. **A:** Are you a student?
   B: Yes, I _____.

2. **A:** What _____ his name?
   B: Sergio.

3. **A:** Are Tim and Donna in the sales department?
   B: No, they _____.

4. **A:** How is your father?
   B: He _____ great.

5. **A:** Is Chicago a small town?
   B: No, it _____.

6. **A:** _____ you ready?
   B: Sure.

7. **A:** My name is Janet.
   B: Hi, Janet. I _____ Carol.

8. **A:** Where _____ your books?
   B: At home.

B. Find and correct the errors in these sentences.

9. It's warm. Opens the window.

10. Meet Dennis. He an employee here.

11. Where your mother is?

12. We're students. We no are teachers.

13. Is interesting the book?

14. I amn't from Mexico.

15. Not drive. Take a taxi.

C. Write an affirmative or negative imperative for each situation. Use the words or phrases in parentheses. Punctuate your sentences correctly.

16. father to child (make/noise)

   _____

17. instructions in a cookbook (add/the milk)

   _____

18. teacher to student (forget/your assignment)

   _____

19. a host to guests (come in/please)

   _____

20. warning label on a bottle (swallow)

   _____

D. Choose the correct situation for each command.

21. Please take the kids to school.
   a. wife to husband
   b. child to parent

22. Use quarters only.
   a. instructions on a test
   b. instructions on a washing machine

23. Listen to this great CD.
   a. friend to friend
   b. warning

24. Turn left at the next corner
   a. bus driver to passenger
   b. passenger to cab driver

25. Open your books.
   a. doctor to patients
   b. teacher to students

4 Introduction to Nouns

FORM

1 Examining Form

Read the conversations and complete the tasks below.

CONVERSATION 1
Rick: Monica says you're in a new <u>house</u>. How is it?
Jada: Beautiful. The place is really nice.
Rick: What's it like?
Jada: Well, the (bedrooms) are large and sunny, and there's a nice living
5   room with a fireplace. And it's in a good neighborhood.
Rick: That sounds great!

CONVERSATION 2
Laura: Do you like your apartment, Josh?
Josh: Not really.
Laura: What's wrong with it?
10   **Josh:** It isn't the building. That's fine. The problem is the neighbors.
There are two men next door. They're musicians, and they're
very noisy.
Laura: That's too bad.

1. Look at the underlined example of a singular noun. Underline seven more.

2. Look at the circled example of a plural noun. Circle three more.

Complete each sentence with the correct form of the noun in parentheses. Add *a* or *an* if necessary.

1. Joe is _an electrician_ (electrician).

2. The _____ (Johnson) are nice neighbors.

3. _____ (studio) in my building is available this month.

4. The young _____ (woman) are on the bus.

5. _____ (car) are expensive.

6. What _____ (country) is Victor from?

7. The _____ (box) aren't very heavy.

8. Are you _____ (tenant) here?

9. How many _____ (person) are here?

10. Fumiko is _____ (student) at the university.

Write the plural form of these nouns and check (✓) the correct pronunciation.

SINGULAR FORM	PLURAL FORM	/s/	/z/	/ɪz/
1. test	tests	✓		
2. watch				
3. soda				
4. map				
5. dorm				
6. book				
7. hotel				
8. office				
9. computer				
10. leader				
11. minute				
12. wish				

MEANING AND USE

4 Identifying Nouns in Sentences

Read the conversation below and think about the meaning and use of the underlined nouns. Then match the underlined nouns to their function.

Denise: What is your name?

Ana: I'm <u>Ana</u>.
_a

Denise: You're <u>a dancer</u>, right?
_b

Ana: Yes, I am <u>a ballerina</u> at <u>the National Theater</u>.
_c _d

Denise: Oh! <u>The National Theater</u> is beautiful.
_e

Ana: Yes, it is. Come and see <u>a performance</u> tomorrow.
_f

Denise: OK. What time?

Ana: At 7:00. Call <u>the theater</u> for <u>tickets</u>.
_g _h

1. noun as subject <u>e</u>

2. noun as object _____ _____

3. noun after *be* _____ _____ _____

4. noun after preposition _____ _____

COMBINING FORM, MEANING, AND USE

5 Thinking About Meaning and Use

Use a noun from the box to complete the conversations. Add *a* or *an* or make the noun plural if necessary.

window	lunch	hour	hill	work	neighbors

1. **A:** When is <u>lunch</u>?
   B: It's at 12:30.

2. **A:** Is the house on _____?
   B: Yes, it is.

3. **A:** Who are they?
   B: The Millers. They're _____.

4. **A:** It's hot in here.
   B: Open _____.

5. **A:** Where is Jackson City?
   B: It's _____ from Denver.

6. **A:** I'm sick.
   B: Don't go to _____ today.

Some of the sentences in this e-mail have errors. Find the errors and correct them.

To: Naomi Green
From: Ruth Banks
Cc:
Subject: Hello

Hi Naomi,

I am back from vacations. We had a great times in Florida. How are you? And how are your childs? Are you happy with your new house? How is your neighbors there?

I am happy at my new job. My bosses is great. The other employee are nice, too. Call me tomorrow evenings. I'm at a home after 7:00.

Ruth

7) **Writing**

Imagine that you are going on vacation. On a separate sheet of paper, make a list of the different items you must pack. Add *a* or *an* or make the noun plural if necessary.

a camera

3 shirts

a map

an umbrella

5 Introduction to Count and Noncount Nouns

FORM

1 Examining Form

Read the list of "kitchen rules" at a student dormitory. Then complete the tasks below.

Kitchen Rules

Welcome to our <u>kitchen</u>! Please follow these (rules):

- Dishes and utensils are on the shelves. Please wash, dry and put back on the shelves.

- Use the liquid detergent in the white plastic bottle.

5 - Throw garbage in the black plastic can. Put glass bottles and aluminum cans in the blue can.

- The coffee and tea in the metal cans are for our guests.

- Throw out your old food. Please don't leave food in the refrigerator!

- Don't use the kitchen after 10:00 P.M.

10 - Please turn off the lights. Help us save electricity.

1. Look at the underlined example of a singular noun. Underline twelve more.

2. Look at the underlined nouns. Write three count and three noncount singular nouns below.

COUNT	NONCOUNT
1. _____	1. _____
2. _____	2. _____
3. _____	3. _____

3. Look at the circled example of a plural noun. Circle nine more.

2 Identifying Count and Noncount Nouns

Read the sentences. Think about the meaning of the underlined words. Write *C* for count nouns and *N* for noncount nouns.

1. __N__ Biology is an interesting subject.

2. _____ Throw the food into the garbage can. It's no good.

3. _____ The ring is large.

4. _____ My hair is very long.

5. _____ Pass me the meat, please.

6. _____ Take the papers to Mr. Davidson.

3 Working on Count and Noncount Nouns

A. Complete each sentence with *is* or *are*.

1. Public transportation __is__ not expensive.

2. The information _____ incorrect.

3. Jeans _____ popular in America.

4. Mathematics _____ a difficult subject for me.

5. This sofa _____ very comfortable.

6. Air pollution _____ unhealthy.

B. Complete each sentence with the correct subject.

1. _____ are never difficult in this class.
   - (a.) Assignments   **b.** Homework

2. _____ is horrible in this part of town.
   - **a.** Traffic   **b.** Cars

3. The new _____ is beautiful.
   - **a.** furniture   **b.** chairs

4. The _____ in our office are ten years old.
   - **a.** copiers   **b.** equipment

5. _____ is always late on Saturdays
   - **a.** Letters   **b.** Mail

6. _____ is very expensive in this store.
   - **a.** Pants   **b.** Clothing

MEANING AND USE

4 **Working on Count and Noncount Nouns**

Choose the correct word or phrase to complete each sentence.

1. The detergent is in (bottle / (a bottle)).

2. Please throw your (paper / a paper) in the trash can.

3. The utensils (is / are) dirty.

4. (Coffee / Coffees) is free for guests.

5. Electricity (are / is) not expensive in my country.

6. Put aluminum (can / cans) in the blue recycling bin.

7. Buy (flours / flour) and eggs for the recipe.

8. Our luggage (are / is) in the car.

9. Please don't waste (water / a water).

10. There is no (glass / glasses) in the windows.

5 **Using Count and Noncount Nouns**

Complete the sentences with a noun from the box. Add *a* or *an* if necessary.

mathematics	friend	weather	litter	knowledge
apple	water	cotton	bike	cup

1. _Cotton_____ is not an expensive material.

2. Get a good education. _____ is important.

3. Don't drive to work. Ride _____ !

4. _____ is my favorite subject at school.

5. The _____ is really bad today. It's cold and rainy.

6. Eat _____ every day. Fruit is good for you.

7. Don't leave garbage outside. _____ is bad for the environment.

8. Save _____. Don't take long showers.

9. Give me _____ of tea, please.

10. Meet Dario. He's _____ .

COMBINING FORM, MEANING, AND USE

6 Thinking About Meaning and Use

Choose the correct words to complete the conversations.

1. **A:** Look at the bracelets.
   B: ____ beautiful.
      a. It's
      b. They're *(circled)*

2. **A:** What's in the bowl?
   B: ____
      a. A soup.
      b. Soup.

3. **A:** Give me ____, please.
   B: Here you are.
      a. pencil
      b. a pencil

4. **A:** ____ is important.
   B: Yes, it is.
      a. Love
      b. A love

5. **A:** What's in the recipe?
   B: ____
      a. Sugar.
      b. A sugar.

6. **A:** How old is Charlie?
   B: He's ____.
      a. teenager
      b. a teenager

7 Writing

On a separate sheet of paper, write a list of six to eight rules or instructions for a place that people use. For example, you can write rules for a hotel, a workplace, a health club, or a home. Put one count or noncount noun in each rule.

> **Library Rules**
> - Don't bring food to the library.
> - Don't write on the books.
> - Return books on time.

Chapters 4–5

A. Complete the sentences with the correct form of the nouns in the box. Add *a* or *an* if necessary.

bracelet	children	paper	football	coffee
sugar	employee	bag	apartment	country

1. Honduras is _____ in Central America.

2. Do you live in _____?

3. The diamond _____ is beautiful.

4. _____ is my favorite drink.

5. Burt is _____ at Compugames.

6. Recycle _____ and glass.

7. Please put the old clothes in _____.

8. _____ is a popular sport in the United States.

9. Don't eat _____. It's bad for your teeth.

10. My _____ are in high school.

B. Choose the best answer to complete each conversation.

11. **A:** Where's the food?
    B: _____
      a. It's in the refrigerator.
      b. They're in the refrigerator.

12. **A:** What's your favorite meat?
    B: _____
      a. Chicken.
      b. A chicken.

13. **A:** Turn off the lights.
    B: _____
      a. Where is it?
      b. Where are they?

14. **A:** Give me _____ please.
    B: Sure. Here are four quarters.
      a. a change
      b. change

15. **A:** Don't waste electricity.
    B: That's right. _____
      a. It's expensive.
      b. They're expensive.

16. **A:** The men are here.
    B: _____
      a. Who is he?
      b. Who are they?

C. Rewrite the sentences as singular or plural. If you cannot change the sentence, write X.

17. Where is your luggage?

_____

18. I'm an engineer.

_____

19. Please bring your books tomorrow.

_____

20. They are beautiful cities.

_____

21. Is the furniture old?

_____

22. It isn't an expensive apartment.

_____

23. The garage is large.

_____

24. Did you get the information?

_____

25. The women aren't doctors.

_____

6 Descriptive Adjectives

FORM

Helen and Ann are at a garage sale. Read the conversation and complete the tasks below.

Helen: How are the clothes?

Ann: They're <u>nice</u>, but they're expensive.

Helen: Look at the old videos! French films from the 50s and 60s!

5 **Ann:** The black belt is nice, but it's large.

Helen: Let me see the belt. Maybe it's my size.

Ann: What's over there?

Helen: Rugs! Oh, look at the oval rug.
10   It's perfect for my bedroom.

Ann: How much is it?

Helen: There's no price on it.

Ann: It's probably expensive.

1. Look at the underlined example of an adjective. Underline nine more.

2. Which adjectives in the conversation come after a noun or a pronoun and a form of *be*?

_____

3. Which adjectives in the conversation come before a noun?

_____

Identifying Adjectives

Circle the adjectives in the sentences. Then draw an arrow to the nouns they describe.

1. The (garage) sale is today.

2. The clothes are cheap.

3. Look at the green dress!

4. The old videos are from the 1950s.

5. How much is the wool jacket?

6. They're beautiful shoes.

7. Is the gold jewelry for sale?

8. Holly is tired and hot.

9. Don't buy the broken TV.

10. The clothing is expensive.

3 **Forming Sentences with Adjectives**

Add the word in parentheses to each sentence. Make all necessary changes.

1. Bob is a man. (tall)

   Bob is a tall man.

2. Meet my sister. (little)

   _____

3. Don't buy a coat. (expensive)

   _____

4. It's a present. (birthday)

   _____

5. Belgium is a country. (small)

   _____

6. Look at my shoes (new)

   _____

7. The ring is from my grandmother. (diamond)

   _____

8. Try the restaurant on Main Street. (Italian)

   _____

MEANING AND USE

4 **Completing Conversations with Descriptive Adjectives**

Circle the correct adjective to complete each conversation.

1. **A:** How's the new apartment?

   B: It's (nice / friendly).

2. **A:** What's your hometown like?

   B: It's (young / small).

3. **A:** Look at the (round / tall) table.

   B: Yes. It's nice.

4. **A:** Are your shoes from Italy?

   B: No, they're (Brazilian / large).

5. **A:** How's dinner?

   B: It's (popular / delicious).

6. **A:** How's the weather in New York?

   B: It's (rainy / strong) today.

5 **Using Nouns as Adjectives**

Complete the sentences with words from the box.

phone	winter	kitchen	chicken
chocolate	cotton	gold	school

1. A __winter__ coat is good for cold weather.

2. The _____ cake is delicious.

3. Let's eat at the _____ table.

4. The red book is from the _____ library.

5. Where's my _____ earring?

6. _____ clothes are cool.

7. Buy a _____ card and call your parents in Argentina.

8. Please make me some _____ soup.

COMBINING FORM, MEANING, AND USE

Match the questions on the left with the answers on the right.

_f_ 1. What are the apartments like?

____ 2. Are Paul and David American?

____ 3. Is your computer new?

____ 4. What color is your dog?

____ 5. How's the weather in Miami?

____ 6. What is the baby like?

____ 7. Is the book good?

____ 8. How's the food?

a. No, it's old.

b. No, it's boring.

c. It's hot and rainy.

d. It's brown and white.

e. It's spicy.

f. They're expensive.

g. He's cute.

h. No. They're Canadian.

7 Writing

A. Answer these questions about something personal that is important to you; for example, a piece of clothing or jewelry, or a piece of furniture.

- What is it?
- Where is it from?
- What's it like? (size, shape, color, age, etc.)
- Why is it important to you?

B. On a separate sheet of paper, write a paragraph about this object.

> My gold bracelet is very important to me. It's Turkish.
> It isn't very old, but it's beautiful. . . .

7 Possessives and Demonstratives

FORM

1 Examining Form

Read the conversations and complete the tasks below.

CONVERSATION 1

Greg: Whose desk is that? Is it (yours)?

John: No, that's my <u>roommate's</u>. Mine is over there. This is my side of the room.

Greg: Are these clothes on the floor his, too?

5 **John:** Well, that's his shirt, but those are my socks.

CONVERSATION 2

Dana: Who are they? Are those the new neighbors?

Robin: Yes, they are.

Dana: What are their names?

Robin: His name is Brad and his wife's is ... Sally, I think. I'm not
10   sure. But their last name is Gilbert. And their children's names
     are Jenny and Mike.

---

1. Look at the underlined example of a possessive noun. Underline two more.

2. One example of *'s* is not a possessive form. Write it here: _____

3. Look at the circled example of a possessive pronoun. Circle two more.

2) Asking and Answering Questions with *Whose*

Use the words and phrases to write the questions to the dialogues. Then use the correct form of the possessive in the answers.

1. whose/dorm/Bigler Hall

   Janet

   A: <u>Whose dorm is Bigler Hall?</u>

   B: <u>It's Janet's.   OR   Janet's.</u>

2. whose/uncle/Mr. Sanborn

   Barry and John

   A: _____

   B: _____

3. whose/house/next door

   the Joneses

   A: _____

   B: _____

4. whose/books/on the desk

   my kids

   A: _____

   B: _____

5. whose/lunch/on the table

   Jonathan

   A: _____

   B: _____

6. whose/gray cat/under the desk

   the manager

   A: _____

   B: _____

3) Working on Possessives and Demonstratives

Complete the conversations. Choose the correct word in parentheses.

1. **A:** (Whose / Who's) shorts are on the bed?
   B: (This / These)? They're Jack's.

2. **A:** (Who's / Whose) the tall man?
   B: (That's / Those are) my brother.

3. **A:** Is (this / these) an apartment building?
   B: No, (it's / its) an office building.

4. **A:** Where are (your / you're) books?
   B: (Their / They're) in my bag.

5. **A:** (This / These) university is beautiful.
   B: Yes. (Its / It's) professors are famous, too.

6. **A:** Is that your (sister's / sisters) car?
   B: No, it's (my / mine).

MEANING AND USE

4 **Working on Possessive Adjectives and Pronouns**

Complete each sentence with a possessive adjective or a possessive pronoun. Do not add any other words.

1. My name is Sandra. What's ___yours___ ?

2. Bill and Derek are in the dorm. _____ room is 517.

3. These aren't my shoes. _____ are red.

4. Celia is Brazilian. _____ family is in São Paulo.

5. Mexico City is a very large city. _____ population is over 15 million.

6. Brad is 16. _____ brother is only 12.

7. Carol, these aren't my gloves. They're _____ .

8. The house is mine and my wife's. It is _____ house.

5 **Identifying the Meaning of Possessives**

A. Read the paragraph below and think about the meaning of each underlined possessive.

> I'm a student at the university, and <u>my</u> room is in a big dormitory. Marta
> Andrews is <u>my</u> roommate. She is a good student. <u>Her</u> grades are excellent. She
> is also pretty and <u>her</u> hair is very long. <u>Marta's</u> brother Paul is a student, too.
> <u>His</u> eyes are blue and he is very handsome.

B. Choose the correct meaning for each underlined word.

1. a. ownership and possession
   b. human relationship

2. a. human relationship
   b. ownership and possession

3. a. ownership and possession
   b. physical characteristics

4. a. ownership and possession
   b. physical characteristics

5. a. physical characteristics
   b. human relationships

6. a. physical characteristics
   b. human relationships

COMBINING FORM, MEANING, AND USE

6 | **Editing**

Each conversation has one error. Find the error and correct it.

1. **A:** Who's that over there?

   B: That's John͵daughter. ⁵

2. **A:** Are that books old?

   B: Yes, they're very old.

3. **A:** Is this your shirt?

   B: Yes, it's my.

4. **A:** Whose pictures are they?

   B: Their Mr. Stewart's.

5. **A:** What's your fathers' first name?

   B: It's Harry.

6. **A:** Is that car Judy's?

   B: No, it's hers brother's.

7 | **Writing**

A. On a separate sheet of paper, draw a family tree. Include as many family members as you can think of.

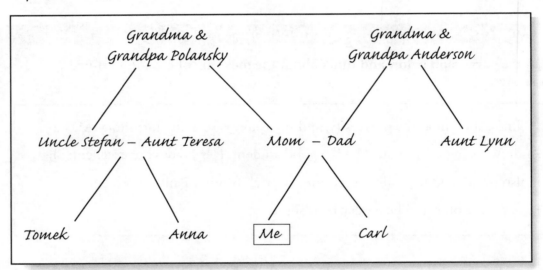

B. Then write a paragraph describing the relationships between the people in your family tree.

> My mother's sister is Aunt Teresa. Her husband is
> Uncle Stefan. They have two children. . . .

Chapters 6–7

A. Use the words and phrases to form questions.

1. birthday / your / today / is

   _____

2. are / like / John's / what / brothers

   _____

3. is / in your country / weather / how

   _____

4. car / blue / is / Amy's

   _____

5. on the table / book / whose / is

   _____

6. leather / where / bag / is / my

   _____

7. OK / pants / these / are

   _____

8. Diane's / Bob / is / husband

   _____

B. Match these answers with the questions in A.

_____ 9. It's in the bedroom.

_____ 10. It's mine.

_____ 11. No, he's my husband.

_____ 12. It's warm.

_____ 13. They're tall and handsome.

_____ 14. Sure, they're fine.

_____ 15. No, hers is white.

_____ 16. No, it's tomorrow.

C. Choose the word or phrase to complete each sentence.

17. The lunch _____ delicious.

    a. are   **b.** is   **c.** am

18. _____ notebooks are these?

    a. Who's   **b.** Whose   **c.** Who is

19. It's _____ old love song.

    a. Ø   **b.** the   **c.** an

20. Look at _____ clothes.

    a. this   **b.** that   **c.** these

21. Is that sweater _____ wool?

    a. Ø   **b.** a   **c.** the

22. This is our _____ room.

    a. daughter   **b.** daughters'   **c.** daughters

23. This is mine and that is _____.

    a. yours   **b.** you're   **c.** your

24. Please don't buy _____ expensive tickets.

    a. an   **b.** a   **c.** Ø

25. _____ parents are nice.

    a. Gary and Susan   **b.** Gary and Susan's   **c.** Gary and Susans'

8   The Present Continuous

FORM

1   Examining Form

Read this e-mail message from Marjorie to her daughter, Gayle. Gayle is a student at college. Then complete the tasks below.

To: Gayle Summer
From: Erica Summer
Cc:
Subject: Hello, dear

---

5   Dear Gayle,

I'm thinking about you a lot this week. How are you doing this semester? And how are your classes going? By the way, are you taking three or four classes? I can't remember. And how is Pete? Is he still taking acting lessons?

10   It's October, but the weather is still hot. I'm still not wearing my fall clothes. Right now I'm wearing just shorts and a t-shirt. Uh-oh, your dad is calling me. He's asking me about dinner.

Please write or e-mail me soon.

Love,
15   Mom

---

1. Look at the underlined example of the present continuous. Underline eight more.

2. Find one example of each of the following present continuous forms:

   a. a *Yes/No* question _____

   b. an information question _____

   c. a negative statement _____

Completing a Conversation with the Present Continuous

David is on a business trip in Hawaii. He is talking on the telephone with his wife, Karen. Use the words and phrases in parentheses to complete the conversation.

David: So, what __'s happening__ (happen) at home?
1

Karen: Nothing much. I _____ (make) dinner right now.
2

David: What _____ (kids/do)?
3

Karen: Well, Robbie _____ (study) for his math test tomorrow.
4

And Dana _____ (watch) TV.
5

David: How's the weather there? _____ (it/still/snow)?
6

Karen: No, not now. It's warmer today. How _____ (you/do)?
7

David: I'm fine. I _____ (relax) right now.
8

Karen: _____ (you/enjoy) your trip?
9

David: Yes. I _____ (work) a lot, but I _____ (enjoy)
10   11

the warm weather.

Karen: That's good. Well, we _____ (think) about you.
12

David: I'll see you soon.

3 **Forming Questions**

Use the words and phrases to write a question for each conversation.

1. who/play/the piano
   A: _Who is playing the piano?_
   B: Holly is.

2. you/drink/coffee
   A: _____?
   B: No, I'm drinking tea.

3. what/Margaret/do/these days
   A: _____?
   B: She's taking an art class.

4. I/make/too much noise
   A: _____?
   B: Yes, you are.

5. how/it/go
   A: _____?
   B: Great, thanks.

6. they/leave/now
   A: _____?
   B: Yes, they are.

7. You/think/about/me
   A: _____?
   B: Yes. I miss you.

8. Luisa/playing/computer games
   A: _____?
   B: No, she's emailing her friend.

MEANING AND USE

Using the Present Continuous to Describe Activities

Write one affirmative and one negative sentence about each picture. Use the present continuous.

1. _The man is waiting for the bus. He is not running._

2. _____

3. _____

4. _____

5. _____

6. _____

5 **Identifying Activities in Progress**

Read each conversation and underline the present continuous verb(s). If the activity is happening at the moment of speaking, write MS in the blank.

1. _MS_ **A:** What <u>are</u> you <u>reading</u>?

B: A mystery novel.

2. _____ **A:** Are you jogging a lot these days?

B: Not much.

3. _____ **A:** Mike, come here!

B: Shh. I'm talking on the phone.

4. _____ **A:** Is Ann still dating Joe?

B: Sometimes.

5. _____ **A:** Where are you working?

B: In a department store.

6. _____ **A:** Is the baby sleeping?

B: Yes, she is.

COMBINING FORM, MEANING, AND USE

Choose the best question to complete each conversation.

1. **A:** _____
   B: Not much.
      a. What are you doing these days?
      b. How are you doing?

2. **A:** _____
   B: At school.
      a. Where is she waiting?
      b. Why is she waiting?

3. **A:** _____
   B: At my parents'.
      a. Where are you going?
      b. Where are you living?

4. **A:** _____
   B: Yes, I am.
      a. Are you working hard?
      b. What is happening?

5. **A:** _____
   B: I'm eating dinner.
      a. Where are you going?
      b. What are you doing?

6. **A:** _____
   B: Your father.
      a. Who's talking?
      b. What's he saying?

7 Writing

On a separate sheet of paper, write a letter or an e-mail message to a relative or a close friend. First ask questions about the other person's activities. Then write several sentences about your own activities.

> Hi Janet,
>
> How are you doing? Are you still having problems with your new job? . . .
>
> I'm studying really hard this semester. I'm taking an advanced science course. . . .

CHAPTER

9 The Simple Present

FORM

Examining Form

Larry and Irina are meeting for the first time at a party. Read the conversation and complete the tasks below.

Larry: So, your name is Irina. That sounds Russian.

Irina: Yes. It means "peace." You have the same name in
5   English—Irene.

Larry: Oh, I see. What do you do?

Irina: I work in a law office in the morning and take classes at the university in the afternoon. What
10   do you do, Larry?

Larry: I teach English in a high school. But I also write novels.

Irina: Oh, that's interesting. Do you write every day?

Larry: No, I don't have much time during the week. I write on weekends.

1. Underline the verbs in all the affirmative statements. What tense do the speakers use? _____

2. Find one example of a negative statement. How is the negative formed?

_____

A. Alex is a college student. Use the words and phrases to make statements about Alex's life. Make all necessary changes.

1. take / Alex / at the university / classes

   Alex takes classes at the university.

2. before 9:00 A.M. / not / he / get up

   _____

3. job / he / have / not

   _____

4. at the pool / swim / every morning / Alex

   _____

5. instrument / play / Alex / musical / a / not

   _____

6. friends / his / near him / live

   _____

7. visit / him / on weekends / they

   _____

8. study / on Sunday night / Alex

   _____

B. Lisa is Alex's older sister. Her life is very different from Alex's. Use the sentences in part A to write about Lisa's life. Change the affirmative statements to negative, and the negative statements to affirmative. Make all necessary changes.

1. Lisa doesn't take classes at the university.

2. _____

3. _____

4. _____

5. _____

6. _____

7. _____

8. _____

MEANING AND USE

Complete the sentences with the correct form of a stative verb from the box.

taste	look	belong	smell	weigh
own	hurt	understand	cost	love

1. Your new ring is great. It _looks_ beautiful.

2. Ken is a heavy man. He _____ over 300 pounds.

3. I don't feel well today. My throat _____.

4. Someone is baking bread. _____ you _____ it?

5. Please repeat that. I _____.

6. The Jensens are rich. They _____ a big house in town and another one in the country.

7. The shirt is only ten dollars. It _____ much.

8. I like these cookies. They _____ great.

9. The care isn't mine. It _____ to my parents.

10. She is my favorite actress. I _____ her movies.

A reporter is interviewing a famous movie actor. Match the interview questions with the answers.

_e_ 1. How many movies do you make a year?

____ 2. Who cooks for you?

____ 3. Do you like to make movies?

____ 4. What time do you get up?

____ 5. Do you have a big house?

____ 6. Does your wife make movies too?

____ 7. Do you use a computer?

____ 8. How often do you go to the movies?

a. No. I live in an apartment.

b. Sure. I send e-mail like everyone else.

c. Different people. I eat in restaurants a lot.

d. Not very much. It's hard work.

e. Two or three.

f. A couple of times a year. I'm too busy.

g. No, she's a teacher.

h. Very early. About 6:00 A.M.

COMBINING FORM, MEANING, AND USE

5 Editing

Some of these sentences have errors. Find the errors and correct them.

Reporter: What subjects ^do^ you study?

Student: I study math, chemistry, and history.

Reporter: Do you taking classes every day?

Student: No, I do take classes four days a week.

Reporter: How many hours a day are you study?

Student: I studying about three hours every day.

Reporter: Where your family does live?

Student: They lives in Japan.

Reporter: Do you visiting them often?

Student: No, I doesn't. I sees them about once a year.

6 Writing

A. Think of a student you know who takes classes and has a job. Think about a typical week in this student's life. Answer these questions.

- What is the student's name?
- What is the name of the university?
- What classes does the student take?
- When does he/she have classes?
- When does he/she study? work? relax?

B. On a separate sheet of paper, write a paragraph about what you do on this day of the week. Look at your notes. Use the simple present.

> I am a student at State University. I take
> classes in English, business, and computer science.
> My classes . . . .

10 Adverbs of Frequency

FORM

1 Examining Form

Betty is from San Francisco. Erica is from New York, but she lives in San Francisco now. Read the conversation and complete the tasks below.

Betty: So how do you like the weather in San Francisco?

Erica: I like it, but it still seems a little strange to me. In New York it's 5 <u>usually</u> hot now. Here it rarely gets hot, even in the middle of summer.

Betty: I know. I love it. And it never rains this time of year. Does it rain in New York in summer?

10 **Erica:** It sometimes does. But we generally get more rain in the spring and the fall.

Betty: Does it snow often in New York?

Erica: Not very often. But we almost always have some snow in January or February.

1. Look at the underlined example of an adverb of frequency. Underline seven more.

2. Find an adverb of frequency that comes after *be*. _____

3. Find two adverbs of frequency that have the same meaning. Write them here:

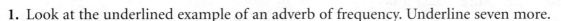

_____

Look at the chart about Bob and Joan's weekend activities. Write sentences about their activities.

ACTIVITY	USUALLY	OFTEN	SOMETIMES	RARELY	NEVER
visit friends			Bob & Joan		
work around the house		Joan		Bob	
get up early				Bob & Joan	
play tennis	Bob				Joan

1. <u>Bob and Joan sometimes visit friends on the weekend.</u>

2. _____

3. _____

4. _____

5. _____

6. _____

Use the words and phrases to complete the conversations. Use correct punctuation.

1. you / dancing / go / ever
   A: <u>Do you ever go dancing?</u>
   B: No, I don't.

2. doesn't / he / work / late / usually
   A: Is Steve still at work?
   B: I don't think so. _____
   _____

3. miss / I / sometimes / my family
   A: Are you ever homesick?
   B: Yes. _____

4. rarely / he / goes out
   A: Do you see Alan a lot?
   B: No, I don't. _____

5. do / how often / milk / you / drink
   A: _____
   B: I drink some almost every day.

6. chocolate / never / I / eat
   A: Take some candy.
   B: No, thanks. _____
   _____

7. sometimes / you / are / lonely
   A: _____
   B: Yes, I am.

8. do / usually / when / eat dinner / you
   A: _____
   B: Around 7:00 P.M.

MEANING AND USE

Rephrasing Sentences

These people have some bad habits. Rewrite each sentence using an adverb of frequency from the box. Do not change the meaning of the sentence. More than one answer is possible.

always	often	rarely
never	usually	almost never

1. Corey eats a lot of junk food.

   Corey often eats junk food.

2. Alan talks on his cell phone all the time.

   _____

3. My brothers don't eat any vegetables.

   _____

4. I hardly ever pay bills on time.

   _____

5. Dana eats breakfast once or twice a year.

   _____

6. Diego and I stay up late most of the time.

   _____

5 **Expressing Opposites**

Rewrite each sentence to express the opposite meaning. Use the subject in parentheses and an adverb of frequency in each new sentence. More than one answer is possible.

1. Bob rarely cooks dinner. (you)

   You often cook dinner.

2. I'm seldom at home. (she)

   _____

3. Dan never eats out. (Brad)

   _____

4. I frequently drink coffee. (Kim)

   _____

5. Keisha always calls me. (Karen)

   _____

6. Sandra is almost never late. (we)

   _____

COMBINING FORM, MEANING, AND USE

Read Josh's paragraph about his weekly activities. Then rewrite the paragraph, using the words in the box in place of the underlined phrases. Make all necessary changes in word order.

always	never	sometimes	rarely	often	generally	occasionally

I am a delivery person. I work four days a week <u>all the time</u>. I <u>frequently</u> work Monday through Thursday. However, <u>some of the time</u> I work Tuesday through Saturday. I <u>hardly ever</u> get overtime. In the evening, I am <u>usually</u> at home with my wife and children. <u>Once in a while</u> I go out alone to visit friends. Those nights I <u>don't ever</u> stay out late. I like to be in bed before midnight.

I am a delivery person. I always work four days a week.

_____

_____

_____

_____

On a separate sheet of paper, write about your typical week or weekend. What do you always do? What do you sometimes do? What do you never do? Use different adverbs of frequency to discuss your activities.

A Typical Weekend

I do the same things on most weekends. On Saturday I usually get up late and have breakfast with my family. In the afternoon I frequently work around the house. . . .

Chapters 8–10

A. Choose the best answer to complete each conversation.

1. **A:** _____
    B: Fine, thanks. And you?
    a. What do you do?
    b. How's it going?
    c. Where are you working?

2. **A:** Are you looking for something?
    B: _____
    a. Yes, we're.
    b. No, I don't.
    c. No, I'm not.

3. **A:** _____
    B: At noon.
    a. Are you eating lunch?
    b. How often do you eat lunch?
    c. When do you usually eat lunch?

4. **A:** How's the weather today?
    B: _____
    a. It's snowing.
    b. It rains.
    c. It's late.

5. **A:** What do you do on Saturdays?
    B: _____
    a. Nothing much.
    b. We're shopping.
    c. Yes, I often do.

6. **A:** Are you studying?
    B: _____
    a. Yes, I study biology.
    b. No, I don't. I watch TV.
    c. No, I'm reading a novel.

7. **A:** Do you always follow the rules?
    B: _____
    a. Well, usually.
    b. Yes, I am.
    c. We never are.

8. **A:** Who lives with you?
    B: _____
    a. Yes, Sara does.
    b. No one. I live alone.
    c. No, not me.

9. **A:** _____
    B: No, please speak louder.
    a. Are you hearing me?
    b. Do you hear me?
    c. What do you hear?

10. **A:** How does the soup taste?
    B: _____
    a. Yes, it does.
    b. It needs more salt.
    c. No, thank you.

B. Rewrite each sentence with a different adverb of frequency. Do not change the meaning. More than one answer is possible.

11. Jackie hardly ever drinks milk.

   _____

12. Do you occasionally drive too fast?

   _____

13. The bus doesn't usually come late.

   _____

14. Bob never stays out after midnight.

   _____

C. Find and correct the errors in these sentences.

15. Does your brother to work?

16. Ana seldom calling me on the weekends.

17. I eating in the cafeteria every day.

18. The children watch TV right now.

19. What you doing these days?

20. Dan remembers seldom his wife's birthday.

21. Does Anita gets good grades?

22. We are save lots of money.

23. Alan doesn't never take the bus.

24. We no take a long vacation every year.

25. Lisa usually study in the library.

11 The Simple Past of *Be*

FORM

1   Examining Form

Read the conversations and complete the tasks below.

CONVERSATION 1

Brad: Hi, John. Welcome back to the office. How <u>was</u> your vacation?

John: It was nice. We were lucky. It usually rains in the mountains this time of year, but the weather was beautiful. Was it busy at the office?

5 **Brad:** No, it wasn't.

CONVERSATION 2

Marcia: Where were you last night? We were over at your house, but you weren't there.

Tamika: I know. We were at the movies. What time were you there?

Marcia: Around 8:30. So, how was the movie?

10 **Tamika:** It wasn't great. The story was silly, and the acting wasn't very good.

---

1. Look at the underlined example of the past tense of *be*. Underline fourteen more.

2. Look again at your underlined examples. Find an example of the each of the following:

   a. affirmative statement   _____

   b. negative statement   _____

   c. *Yes/No* question   _____

   d. short answer   _____

   e. information question   _____

   f. answer to information question _____

2 Working on Simple Past Statements with *Be*

Complete the paragraph about ziggurats with *was* or *were*.

The Ziggurat at Ur, Iraq

Ziggurats ___were___ large towers in Mesopotamia. Mesopotamia _____ an
                    1   2

ancient land between the Tigris and the Euphrates Rivers in the Middle East. Ziggurats

_____ similar to the pyramids of Egypt. However, they _____ not tombs like
          3   4

the pyramids. They _____ religious buildings. A small temple or sanctuary
                   5

_____ at the top of a ziggurat.
6

3 Writing Questions

Use the words and phrases to write questions with *was* or *were*. Punctuate your
sentences correctly.

1. you / busy / yesterday

A: _Were you busy yesterday?_

B: No, I wasn't.

2. where / Daniel's parents / born

A: _____

B: In France.

3. Mozart / a philosopher

A: _____

B: No, he was a composer.

4. what / the play / like?

A: _____

B: It was really good.

5. when / you and your wife / in London

A: _____

B: In May.

6. who / that

A: _____

B: That was George. He's someone from
work.

MEANING AND USE

Match the questions on the left with the answers on the right.

_d_ **1.** Was Napoleon Spanish?   **a.** Yes, she was.

_____ **2.** Who was the first U.S. president?   **b.** An ancient tribe in Mexico.

_____ **3.** What was the occupation of Marie Curie? **c.** In India.

_____ **4.** Where was Mahatma Gandhi born?   **d.** No, he was French.

_____ **5.** Was Joan of Arc a woman?   **e.** She was a scientist.

_____ **6.** Who were the Aztecs?   **f.** George Washington.

A. Use the words and phrases to make questions with *was* and *were*. Punctuate your sentences correctly.

1. you / born / when / were

   When were you born?

2. happy / were / child / you / a

   _____

3. three / ago / you / years / were / where

   _____

4. sick / were / you / week / last

   _____

5. short / hair / year / your / was / last

   _____

6. last / teacher / English / was / who / your

   _____

7. a student / you / last / were / year

   _____

8. grade / friend / in / was / school / your / who / best

   _____

B. Now answer the questions in part A with a partner. Give true information about yourself.

COMBINING FORM, MEANING, AND USE

Complete the sentences below with *was* or *were* and a word or phrase from the box. Choose the word or phrase that matches the meaning in parentheses.

in school	born in Russia	delicious
cloudy	a waiter	comfortable

1. (origin) My grandparents _were born in Russia_____.

2. (occupation) Five years ago George _____.

3. (characteristic) My old couch _____.

4. (state or condition) The weather _____ yesterday.

5. (location) _____ you _____ yesterday?

6. (characteristic) The cookies _____.

A. Think about the answers to these questions about a friend from childhood.

- What was your friend's name?
- When and where were you friends?
- Were you very close friends?
- What was your friend like?
- What was your friend's family like?

B. On a separate sheet of paper, write a paragraph about your friend. Use your answers from part A to help you.

> My best friend from my childhood was Adam.
> Adam and I were friends in elementary school. We were
> very close. ...

An

12 The Simple Past

FORM

1 Examining Form

Read the article about changing fashions in men's beards and complete the tasks below.

Beards through the Ages: 1500s to 1960

Handlebar Mustache

From the 1500s to about the 1700s, beards and mustaches <u>were</u> sometimes fashionable and sometimes unfashionable in different

10 European countries. Often the king of a country decided the fashion for his people. For example, Henry VIII wore a beard in the late 1530s, so beards were fashionable in England

15 at that time.

In the 1700s, beards were not popular in most of Europe. In Russia Peter the Great even passed a law against beards. In the 1700s, most

20 upper-class men used wigs and didn't grow beards.

In the 1800s, beards and mustaches were fashionable again. Many men grew full beards. Some

25 grew very long mustaches and curled them at the ends. They called these "handlebar" mustaches because they looked like the handlebar of a bicycle.

30 Between 1920 and the early 1960s, not many men in Europe or America wore beards. A beard became the sign of a different or unusual person, such as an artist

35 or a writer. Then in the late 1960s, more and more young men grew beards. They grew long hair and didn't shave. And once again beards came back into

40 fashion.

1. Look at the underlined example of the affirmative simple past. Underline sixteen more.

   Which are regular? _____

   Which are irregular? _____

   _____

2. Find three negative past-tense forms and write them here. _____

   _____

2) Working on Simple Past Verbs

A. Write the simple past forms of these regular verbs and check (✓) the correct pronunciation.

BASE FORM	SIMPLE PAST FORM	/d/	/t/	/ɪd/
1. look	looked		✓	
2. want				
3. use				
4. invent				
5. call				
6. watch				

B. Write the simple past forms of these irregular verbs.

1. catch __caught__

2. come _____

3. drive _____

4. find _____

5. go _____

6. hear _____

7. meet _____

8. see _____

9. speak _____

10. teach _____

11. think _____

12. win _____

3) Working on Simple Past Statements

Use the words and phrases to make statements. Change all the verbs to simple past.

1. people / put / powder / in the 1700s / in their hair

   In the 1700s people put powder in their hair.

2. not wear / beards / they / mustaches / or

   _____

3. Napoleon Bonaparte / have / of gloves / hundreds

   _____

4. not show / women / their / Victorian / legs

   _____

5. suits / top hats / and / men / working class / not wear

   _____

6. fashionable / beards / again / become / in the late 1960s

   _____

MEANING AND USE

Matching Answers to Simple Past Questions

Match the questions on the left to the answers on the right.

_d_ 1. Did you work last Friday?

_____ 2. Where did the kids go yesterday?

_____ 3. Who found my gloves?

_____ 4. What did you do in New York?

_____ 5. Did Queen Victoria wear a wig?

_____ 6. What happened in school?

a. David.

b. To the mall.

c. The teacher gave us a test.

d. Yes, I did.

e. No, she didn't.

f. We went to the theater.

Talking About Situations in the Past

Complete each conversation with a verb from the box. Use the affirmative or negative form of the simple past in each example.

Conversation 1

stay	go	get	happen	call	feel

A: What ___happened___ to you yesterday?
              1

B: I _____ well, so I _____ in bed all day.
           2   3

A: _____ you _____ a doctor?
          4   4

B: No, but I _____ to the Health Center this morning.
                     5

   I _____ some medication.
        6

Conversation 2

enjoy	eat	rent	do	be	see

A: Hi, Lisa. How _____ your vacation?
                         1

B: Great. We really _____ it.
                            2

A: _____ you _____ anything special?
          3   3

B: Yes. We _____ a room in a hotel in Chicago for a week.
                   4

   We _____ a great exhibit at the art museum and _____ in
         5   6

some excellent restaurants.

COMBINING FORM, MEANING, AND USE

6 Understanding Meaning and Use

A. Mark Twain was an American writer. Read this timeline, which shows important events in Mark Twain's life. Underline all of the simple past verbs.

	YEAR	EVENT
1.	1835	<u>was</u> born in Florida, Missouri
2.	1839	moved with his family to Hannibal, Missouri
3.	1861	went to the Nevada Territory with his brother
4.	1864	met the writer Bret Harte in San Francisco
5.	1870	married Olivia Langdon
6.	1877	wrote *The Adventures of Huckleberry Finn*, his best novel
7.	1884	started his own publishing company
8.	1910	died in Hartford, Connecticut

B. Use the information in the chart to write the missing questions and answers. Write full sentences.

1. **A:** <u>When was Mark Twain born?</u>

   B: Mark Twain was born in 1835.

2. **A:** Where did he move in 1839?

   B: _____

3. **A:** _____

   B: To the Nevada Territory.

4. **A:** _____

   B: The writer Bret Harte.

5. **A:** When did he marry Olivia Langdon?

   B: _____

6. **A:** _____

   B: No, he didn't. He wrote it in 1877.

7. **A:** _____

   B: He started his own publishing company.

8. **A:** When did he die?

   B: _____

7 Writing

On a separate sheet of paper, write about one day last week. Was it a typical day or an unusual day? What happened? Describe the day in detail.

> Last Tuesday was an interesting day for me. I didn't work. I took my family to the zoo in the morning. . . .

13 The Past Continuous

FORM

 1 **Examining Form**

Read the newspaper article and complete the tasks below.

Earthquake Reactions

This week our on-the-street reporter talked with people about Tuesday's 6:45 A.M. earthquake. His question was: "What <u>were</u> you <u>doing</u> during the earthquake?"

5 "I was taking a shower and singing. I felt a little shake, but I didn't hear any noise. I was probably making too much noise myself."
Robert, 63, salesman

10 "I was making breakfast in the kitchen. The kids were sitting at the breakfast table. We got a little scared, but it was over in a few seconds."
15 **Sally, 35, teacher**

"I was going to work. I was listening to the news on the radio. I didn't notice anything because I was driving."
20 **Miguel, 27, computer technician**

"I was still sleeping. It woke me up. After I woke up, I looked up at the lamp on the ceiling. It was still moving."
25 **Dan, 16, high school student**

1. Look at the underlined example of the past continuous. Underline ten more.

2. What two forms of the past continuous did you find? _____

3. Find the sentence that contains both the simple past and the past continuous.

Write it here. _____

Working on Past Continuous Statements

Look at the pictures. What were these people doing last night at 7:00 P.M.? Use the words and phrases to write an affirmative or a negative sentence about each picture. Use the past continuous.

1. sing

Betty and Linda _were singing._

3. watch TV

Brad _____

2. read a book

Sue _____

4. play a video game

Tom and I _____

Describing a Scene in a Story

Use the words and phrases to write a sentence to begin each story. Change the verbs to the past continuous.

1. (take the dog / I / for a walk)

  I was taking the dog for a walk. All of a sudden, we heard an ambulance.

2. (ride / Rick / in an elevator)

  _____ Suddenly, the lights went out.

3. (and I / my brother / to the beach / drive)

  _____ Then I saw the police car behind me.

4. (airplane passengers / the / dinner / have)

  _____ Suddenly, the captain made an announcement.

MEANING AND USE

4 **Contrasting the Simple Past and the Past Continuous**

Complete this paragraph about an unusual event. Use the simple past or the past continuous form of the verbs in parentheses.

It _____was_____ (be) late on a stormy Thursday night. The wind _____ (blow)
        1   2
hard. My wife and I _____ (sit) in the living room. We _____ (watch) a
                              3   4
movie on TV. Our children _____ (sleep). Suddenly I _____ (hear) a
                                        5   6
strange noise, so I _____ (get up) and _____ (look) out the window. I
                          7   8
_____ (see) a bright flash of lightning. The lightning _____ (hit) the
     9   10
big tree in our front yard. There _____ (be) a loud crash, and the tree
                                          11
_____ (fall) to the ground.
     12

5 **Conversations with the Present Simple and Past Continuous**

Complete the conversations with the verbs in the box. Use the past continuous or the simple past.

Conversation 1

do   call   sleep   watch

A: (you) _Were you sleeping_ when I _____ last night?
                          1   2
B: No, I wasn't.

A: What (you) _____?
                          3
B: I _____ TV.
            4

Conversation 2

see   shop   not see   go

A: I _____ you downtown yesterday morning.
            1
B: Really? I _____ you.
                        2
A: (you) _____ to work?
                    3
B: No, I _____.
                    4

COMBINING FORM, MEANING, AND USE

6 **Editing**

The *Titanic* sank on April 12, 1912. It was a horrible ship disaster. Read the sentences about the disaster. Some of the sentences have errors. Find the errors and correct them.

    The *Titanic* was ~~make~~ making its first trip across the Atlantic. It is sailing from Southampton to New York City. Over 2,200 people were traveled on the ship. Many of the passengers slept in their cabins. The ship were going too fast in dangerous waters. The crew wasn't seeing the iceberg. The ship hit the iceberg. The *Titanic* was sinking to the bottom of the ocean.

7 **Writing**

On a separate sheet of paper, write about a time when you first heard about an important event. Say what the event was. Then explain your situation when you heard the news. Where were you? Were you working? relaxing? studying? Use the past continuous and simple past correctly.

> In 1998 my grandfather died. My father called me and told me the sad news. I was cleaning my apartment. It was a nice day outside and the sun was shining. . . .

Chapters 11–13

A. Choose the correct answer to complete each conversation.

1. **A:** What happened yesterday?
   B: _____
   a. I got sick.
   b. Nothing was.
   c. No, it wasn't.

2. **A:** Were you sleeping?
   B: No, _____
   a. I rested.
   b. I was resting.
   c. I rest.

3. **A:** _____
   B: No, I wasn't.
   a. What did you do last night?
   b. Where were you last night?
   c. Were you at home last night?

4. **A:** What _____
   B: A long dress.
   a. she wore?
   b. did she wear?
   c. she was wearing?

5. **A:** What were you doing when I called?
   B: I _____
   a. watch TV.
   b. watched TV.
   c. was watching TV.

6. **A:** How did you get to the airport?
   B: _____
   a. After 6 p.m.
   b. We took a taxi.
   c. I think so.

7. **A:** Was Renoir a composer?
   B: _____. He was a painter.
   a. No, he wasn't.
   b. I don't know.
   c. That's right.

8. **A:** _____ at the library this morning?
   B: No, I was studying at home.
   a. You were
   b. Were you
   c. Did you

9. **A:** What were you doing there?
   B: _____
   a. Nothing.
   b. No, I wasn't.
   c. None.

10. **A:** _____
    B: In 1989.
    a. What happened?
    b. When did you move?
    c. Where did he graduate?

B. Match the questions on the left with the response on the right.

_____ 11. What was the movie like?   **a.** They laughed.

_____ 12. Who came to the meeting?   **b.** No, I was working

_____ 13. What did they do then?   **c.** Ten minutes ago.

_____ 14. Were you at Carol's party?   **d.** We traveled by train.

_____ 15. How did you get to Boston?   **e.** It was great

_____ 16. When did Brian leave?   **f.** Tom and Rita.

C. Find and correct the errors in these sentences.

17. I born in 1979.

18. Sara not enjoyed the play.

19. Why wasn't you call me last night?

20. I no finish my homework last night.

21. Who did send the letter?

22. When you woke up this morning?

23. I was cleaning house while you resting.

24. Bill and I was good friends in high school.

25. Was John win the prize yesterday?

14 Articles

FORM

Louise is talking with Doris about her vacation. Read the conversation and complete the tasks below.

Doris: Hi, Louise. How was your vacation in Quebec?

Louise: We had(a)great trip.

Doris: Quebec sounds like an
5   interesting place to visit.

Louise: It was. Especially Quebec City.

Doris: What's <u>the</u> city like?

Louise: Well, it has(an)old part and(a)
         new part. <u>The</u> old part is up on
10   (a)cliff, above <u>the</u> river. Most of <u>the</u>
         really interesting old buildings
         are up there. But <u>the</u> new part
         is interesting too.

Doris: Did you have(a)map and(a)
15   guidebook?

Louise: We did. <u>The</u> map was useful, but <u>the</u>
         guidebook wasn't very good. It was old
         and the information was out of date.

Map labels: Kuujjuaq, Inoucdjouac, Schefferville, QUEBEC, Labrador City, Sept-Iles, Comeau, Chibougamau, Chicoutimi, Noranda, Quebec City, Montreal

1. Look at the circled example of an indefinite article (*a, an*). Circle six more. When do we use *a* and when do we use *an*?

   _____

2. Look at the underlined example of a definite article. Underline seven more.

3. Write an example of each of the following:
   a. *the* + singular count noun   _____
   b. *the* + noncount noun   _____
   c. *the* + plural count noun   _____

A. Rewrite the sentences. Change the singular nouns to plural nouns. Where no change is possible, write an X.

1. Buy a ticket here.   <u>Buy tickets here.</u>

2. The movie was interesting.   <u>The movies were interesting</u>

3. Did you read the information?   _____

4. A house is expensive.   <u>A houses are expensive</u>

5. I saw a tourist in the city.   <u>I saw tourists in the city.</u>

6. We drank the milk.   _____

B. Rewrite the sentences. Change the plural nouns to singular nouns. Make any necessary changes.

1. The chairs are comfortable.   <u>The chair is comfortable.</u>

2. It's easy to find good restaurants.   <u>It's easy to find a good restaurant.</u>

3. Stay home on rainy days.   <u>Stay home a rainy day.</u>

4. I ate eggs for breakfast.   <u>I ate an egg for breakfast.</u>

5. We often take taxis.   <u>We often take a taxi.</u>

6. Give me the suitcases.   <u>Give me the suitcas.</u>

3 **Choosing the Correct Article**

Choose the correct article to complete each sentence. More than one answer may be possible.

1. _____ houses in this neighborhood are beautiful.

   a. a   **b.** an   **c.** the ⃝

2. We found _____ earring on the ground.

   a. a   **b.** an   **c.** the

3. I need _____ milk for my coffee.

   a. Ø   **b.** the   **c.** a

4. We waited for _____ hour.

   a. an   **b.** Ø   **c.** a

5. _____ teacher came to class late.

   a. an   **b.** the   **c.** Ø

6. Sara likes _____ ballroom dancing.

   a. a   **b.** Ø   **c.** the

MEANING AND USE

Use the words and phrases to complete the conversations. Add an article where necessary, and make any other necessary changes.

1. Jack / have / new car

   A: Jack has a new car.

   B: What kind of car is it?

2. trip / be / great

   A: Did you enjoy your trip?

   B: Yes. _____

3. you / want / glass of water

   A: _____

   B: No, thanks. I'm not thirsty.

4. I / like / video games

   A: _____

   B: I like them, too.

5. who / be / letter / from

   A: You got a letter.

   B: _____

6. I / go to / museum

   A: _____

   B: Which museum did you go to?

Complete the conversations with *a*, *an*, *the*, or Ø.

Conversation 1

A: Do you live in _an_ apartment?
        1

B: No, I live in ____ house.
                    2

A: How's ____ neighborhood there?
            3

B: ____ neighborhood is fine, but ____ schools are not very good.
       4   5

Conversation 2

A: I went to ____ new play last night.
                1

B: Oh really? What was ____ play about?
                          2

A: It was about ____ two men who are in love with one woman.
                   3

B: ____ love triangle! That's ____ new play, but ____ old story!
       4   5   6

Conversation 3

A: Do you have ____ children?
                  1

B: Yes, I do. I have ____ boy and ____ girl.
                        2   3

A: How old is ____ boy?
                 4

B: He's ten, and ____ girl is eight.
                    5

COMBINING FORM, MEANING, AND USE

6 Editing

Some of the sentences in the postcard message have errors. Find the errors and correct them.

Dear Julia,
Istanbul is ~~the~~ *a* wonderful city!
I really love ~~an~~ old buildings and ~~a~~
wonderful markets. Yesterday I
bought beautiful leather jacket for
the great price. I'm sorry we're only
staying for week!

       Love,

       Mary

Julia Anderson
245 S. Oak St.
Los Angeles, CA 90012
USA

7 Writing

Choose one of these three items: a car, a cell phone, or a computer. On a separate sheet of paper, explain why the item is useful in daily life. Give details on how it is useful. Use specific examples.

> I think a computer is very useful in daily life. We use computers at work and at home. We can e-mail with family on a computer and find information on the Internet. . . .

15 Quantity Expressions

FORM

Read the conversation and complete the tasks below.

Ana: You look great, Kyle. Do you pay attention to your diet?

Kyle: Yes, I do. I eat <u>a lot of</u> (vegetables).

Ana: Do you eat any meat? Or are you
5   a vegetarian?

Kyle: I'm not a vegetarian. I don't eat red meat, but I have some chicken and fish each week. Actually, I love fish. It's very good for you.

10 **Ana:** I know. I try to eat some fish every week, too. But I don't eat many vegetables because I don't like them.

1. Look at the statements with quantity expressions. Underline the quantity expressions and circle the nouns that follow them. Look at the first example. Find three more.

2. Which of the circled nouns are singular and which are plural?

   Singular: _____

   Plural: _____

3. Find the question that contains a quantity expression. Write the quantity expression

   and the noun that follows it. _____

Choosing Quantity Expressions

Choose the correct quantity expression to complete each sentence.

1. Do you drink (much / many) milk?

2. Some vegetarians don't eat (any / some) fish.

3. Sally puts (a lot of / much) syrup on her pancakes.

4. Could I have (a little / a few) more coffee, please?

5. How (many / much) eggs do you want for breakfast?

6. We only have (a little / a few) potatoes left.

7. I often have (some / any) fruit for dessert.

8. David is a growing teenager. He eats (a lot / a lot of).

9. We brought (many / much) books to the class.

10. Give her (any / some) money.

Working on Quantity Expressions

Complete each conversation with a quantity expression from the box.

a few	any	much	a little	many	no

1. **A:** I need some money.
   B: How _much_ do you need?

2. **A:** Are you ready?
   B: No. I need _a few_ more minutes.

3. **A:** Was the supermarket crowded?
   B: Oh yes! There were _____ people there.

4. **A:** Can you give me a stamp?
   B: Sorry. I don't have _____.

5. **A:** How about some more soup?
   B: Thanks. Just _____.

6. **A:** Do you want our couch?
   B: No thanks. We have _____ space for it.

MEANING AND USE

4) Rephrasing Sentences

Rewrite the sentences below. Replace the underlined words with another quantity expression, but do not change the meaning.

1. I need <u>a little</u> help with my homework.

   I need some help with my homework.

2. We aren't making <u>a lot of</u> progress today.

   We aren' making much progress today.

3. Danny drinks *a lot of* <u>cups and cups of</u> coffee every morning.

4. I have *a few* <u>one or two</u> ideas. *few mean 1 or 2 or 3*

5. Dana gave me *a few* <u>some</u> good suggestions.

6. We need to buy *some* <u>a little</u> food for dinner.

7. Did you make *a lot of* <u>many</u> mistakes on the test?

8. Bill doesn't have *much* <u>a lot of</u> patience.

5) Using Quantity Expressions

Complete each sentence with a quantity expression and a noun. Use your imagination.

1. My friends saw <u>a lot of interesting movies last summer.</u>

2. Rich people don't have _____

3. I ate _____

4. Karen speaks _____

5. Barbara and Alan didn't spend _____

6. We don't need _____

COMBINING FORM, MEANING, AND USE

6 Understanding Meaning and Use

Match the questions on the left with the answers on the right.

_d_ **1.** How many people were at the meeting?

_f_ **2.** Do you want some milk in your coffee?

_a_ **3.** How much did the dinner cost?

_e_ **4.** Do you have any pets?

_e_ **5.** Does your city get a lot of tourists?

_b_ **6.** Did you do any work yesterday?

a. Not much. It was cheap.

b. Yes, we did a lot.

c. It gets some.

d. Just a few. My boss, the secretary, and me.

e. No, I don't have any.

f. Yes, please. Just a little.

7 Writing

A. Answer the questions about your health habits in the survey.

Health Survey

1. Do you eat a good breakfast?

    a. Yes, every day.   **b.** A few times a week.   **c.** No, never.

2. Do you eat a lot of fruit and vegetables?

    a. Yes, I do.   **b.** Yes, some.   **c.** No, not many.

4. How often do you exercise?

    a. Every day.   **b.** A few days a week.   **c.** Never.

5. How much sleep do you get?

    a. A lot.   **b.** Not a lot.   **c.** Only a few hours every day.

B. On a separate sheet of paper, write a paragraph about your health habits. Use information from the survey.

> I think I have good health habits. I eat a good breakfast every day. Also, I eat a lot of fruit and vegetables. . . .

16 *There Is* and *There Are*

FORM

1 Examining Form

Read this excerpt from a tourist guide to New Orleans, Louisiana and complete the tasks below.

Transportation in New Orleans

The Regional Transit Authority (RTA) operates public transportation in New Orleans. There
5 are seventy (bus lines) and two (streetcar) (lines). There is no subway. The St. Charles streetcar line runs from the French Quarter to the Garden
10 District, and it is a favorite with visitors.

There are several private tour companies that provide bus tours of New Orleans. Contact the visitor
15 center on Jackson Square for schedules and information.

There are ships that offer cruises on the Mississippi River. The 11:30 A.M. cruise on the
20 *Natchez* is a popular river trip. The cruise takes about two hours. There is also a dinner cruise on the *Natchez*.

Some visitors like to see the city
25 from a horse-drawn carriage. The carriages are available every day at Jackson Square. But be careful! There are not many city laws about the operation of
30 these carriages. So prices and service can vary.

---

1. Underline all the examples of *there is* and *there are*. Circle the nouns they refer to. Look at the first example. Find five more.

2. Look again at the examples you underlined. Which two are negative? How are these examples different from one another? _____

_____

3. Rewrite the sentence with *no*. Use *not* in place of *no*.

_____

2 Affirmative and Negative Statements with *There Is/There Are*

A. Use the words and phrases to make affirmative statements with *there is/there are*. Change the order of the words if necessary.

1. on this street/a bus line <u>There's a bus line on this street.</u>

2. some flowers/in the garden _____

3. in the refrigerator/a little food _____

4. rectangles/in the painting _____

B. Write two negative statements for each affirmative statement in Part A.

1. <u>There's no bus line on this street. There isn't a bus line on this street.</u>

2. _____

3. _____

4. _____

3 Working on Questions with *There Is/There Are*

Use the words and phrases to write questions with *there is/there are*.

1. any museums/in your town

   A: <u>Are there any museums in your town?</u>

   B: Yes, there are two.

2. how many books/in the library

   A: How many books are in the library

   B: I have no idea.

3. an easy solution/to the problem

   A: Is there an easy solution to the problem

   B: No, there isn't.

4. how much sugar/in this dessert

   A: How much sugar is in this dessert.

   B: About a cup.

5. much traffic/in the afternoon

   A: How much traffic is in the morning

   B: Not too much.

6. any good restaurants/in the neighborhood

   A: Is there any good restaurants ino the neighborhood

   B: Yes. There's one around the corner.

MEANING AND USE

4 **Describing a Picture**

Look at the picture of the park. Then look at the words below and circle the things you don't see in the picture.

ducks	fountain	jogger	flowers	trees	gardener	dogs	snake

Write an affirmative or negative sentence with *there is/there are* and each of the words above.

1. <u>There are two ducks.</u>   5. _____

2. _____   6. _____

3. _____   7. _____

4. _____   8. _____

5 **Asking and Answering Factual Questions**

Use the words and phrases to write questions and answers with *there is/there are*. If the fact is incorrect, write the correct answer.

1. eight days in a week

   A: <u>Are there eight days in a week?</u>

   B: <u>No. There are seven days.</u>

2. a leap year every three years

   A: _____

   B: _____

3. ten dimes in a dollar

   A: _____

   B: _____

4. 55 minutes in an hour

   A: _____

   B: _____

5. full moon every month

   A: _____

   B: _____

6. 54 weeks in a year

   A: _____

   B: _____

COMBINING FORM, MEANING, AND USE

Some of the sentences in this student's composition have errors. Find the errors and correct them.

Transportation in My City

    I live in a large city. There ~~are~~ *is* a public transportation system in my city, but it isn't always easy or convenient to use. There a subway system, but the subway lines only go through part of the city. There are many bus line. But the buses are often crowded. There was streetcars in the past, but there no are any streetcars now.

    Most people in my city prefer to travel by car. People drive on the city streets or drive on the freeways. There is very large freeway system. The freeways go almost everywhere in the city. But the freeways aren't always convenient because there are a lot of traffic.

On a separate sheet of paper, write a paragraph about transportation in your city or town. Use *there is* and *there are*. Use the questions below to help you.

- Is there a public transportation system in your town?
- Are there many buses?
- Are there streetcars?
- Do most people use public transportation or travel by car?

>   I live in New York City. There is public transportation in New York City. There is a subway and there are buses. . . .

Chapters 14–16

A. Choose the correct word or phrase to complete each sentence.

1. **A:** Are there any eggs in the recipe?
   B: Yes, _____
   a. there are
   b. they are
   c. there is

2. **A:** Do you have pets?
   B: Yes, I do. I have _____ cat. _singular count noun._
   a. Ø
   b. a
   c. the

3. **A:** Do you speak any French?
   B: No, not _____.
   a. a few
   b. a little
   c. much

4. **A:** I'd like to ask a question.
   B: I'm sorry. There's _____ time for questions.
   a. any
   b. few
   c. no _or not_

5. **A:** What does your father do?
   B: He's _____ architect.
   a. a
   b. an
   c. the

6. **A:** Do you have _____ friends here?
   B: Yes, I do.
   a. a lot of
   b. a lot
   c. much

7. **A:** Where's _____ train station? *[handwritten: spacific]*

   B: It's in the next block.

   (a.) the

   b. a

   c. Ø

8. **A:** Do you have homework? *[handwritten: noncount noun]*

   B: Yes, _____.

   (a.) a lot

   b. a lot of

   c. many →

B. Find and correct the errors in these sentences.

9. How many traffic is there in your town? *[handwritten: much → noncout noun]*

10. There are much people in the park. *[handwritten: many → count noun]*

11. Hurry up! The movie is starting in a little minutes. *[handwritten: few → quatity]*

12. Small towns don't usually have a department stores. *[handwritten: plurl, not need Article]*

13. It's a good idea to get map in a new city. *[handwritten: a sing]*

14. The neighborhood doesn't have a lot restaurants. *[handwritten: of]*

C. Complete the conversation with words in the box.

some	much	a	how much	a lot of	there is
how many	there are	a little	the		is there

John: I'm going to ___the___ supermarket. Do you want anything?
    15

Karen: Hmm. I don't think we need ___much___. Let me look in the refrigerator.
    16

   We only have ___a little___ milk. Get ___a___ carton of milk.
    17   18

John: OK. ___How much___ bread do we have? ___Is There___ enough?
    19   20

Karen: ___There is___ enough bread for now.
    21

John: How about fruit? I eat ___a lot of___ fruit on this new diet. *[handwritten: noncount noun]*
    22

Karen: ___There are___ three apples and two pears. We need ___some___ more
    23   24

   fruit. How about oranges?

John: OK. ___How many___?
    25

17 The Future with *Be Going To*

FORM

1 ▸ Examining Form

Read this newspaper article and complete the tasks below.

On-the-Street Interviews

This week our reporter talked with people about their plans for the championship football game this weekend. His question: What are you going to do Supergame weekend?

"My wife and I <u>are going to watch</u>
5 the game with some friends. We're going to enjoy it on our big-screen TV."

Larry, 32, sales executive

"I feel really lucky because I have
10 tickets for the game. I'm going to fly to St. Louis to watch the game in person."

Dave, 29, accountant

"I have to work that day, so I'm not
15 going to watch the game. I feel sorry about that."

Robert, 50, cook

"My husband and I are going to be at home. I want to watch the game, but
20 he's not a sports fan, so he's not going to watch it with me. He's going to do something else."

Marjorie, 45, hairstylist

---

1. Look at the underlined example of the affirmative form of the future with *be going to*. Underline four more examples.

2. Look at the circled example of the negative form of the future with *be going to*. Circle another example.

3. How do we form an information question with the future with *be going to*? Find an example of an information question with the future with *be going to*.

_____

_____

Use the words and phrases to make affirmative and negative statements with *be going to.*

1. the big game / be / this weekend

   The big game is going to be this weekend.

2. the Lions / play / the Bears

   The lions are going to play the Bears.

3. the Lions / not win / the championship

   The Lions aren't going to win the championship.

4. I / buy / my tickets / online

   I am going to buy my tickets online.

5. our friends / not go / to the game / with us

   Our friends aren't going to go to the game with us

6. they / meet / us / before the game

   They are going to meet us before the game.

7. we / take / food / for a picnic

   We are going to take food for a picnic

8. we / not be / home / late

   We aren't going to be home late.

3 **Working on Questions with *Be Going To***

Use the words and phrases to write questions with *be going to* in the conversations.
Punctuate your sentences correctly.

1. what time / Barry / arrive

   A: What time is Barry going to arrive?

   B: At eight o'clock.

2. you / baseball game / tomorrow / watch

   A: Are you going to watch baseball game tomorrow?

   B: Yes, I am.

3. who / come / for dinner / on Thursday

   A: Who is going to come for dinner on Thursday?

   B: Bob and Alice.

4. it / rain / this weekend

   A: Is it going to rain this weekend.

   B: I don't think so.

5. how / you / get / to the airport

   A: How are you going to get to the airport.

   B: I'm going to call a taxi.

6. who / join / the Red Sox / next year

   A: Who is going to join the Red Sox next year

   B: My favorite player—Ken Robson.

MEANING AND USE

Writing About Future Plans

Complete these sentences in a logical way. Use the future with *be going to*. Write at least one negative statement.

1. After class today my friends and I _are going to see a movie._

2. Next summer I _am going to travel to Hawaii_

3. Tomorrow afternoon I _am going to shop_ .

4. Next weekend my friends and I _are going to_

5. Next year I _am going to buy a new phone_

6. On the next rainy day I _am going to outside._

Making Predictions

Look at the pictures. Make predictions about what is going to happen. Write one affirmative and one negative prediction for each picture.

1.

The car isn't going to stop in time.
The car is going to crash.

3.

He is going to score a goal.!
The goalie is not going to catch the ball.

2.

He is not going to see the rock.
They are going to fall.

4.

The dog is not going to catch the cat.
The cat is going to climb the tree.
The dog is going to get the cat

COMBINING FORM, MEANING, AND USE

6) Editing

Read this note from George to Karl. Some of the sentences have errors. Find the errors and correct them.

> Hi Karl,
>
> I need to ask you some questions about the game on Saturday. Am I going to
> ~~driving~~ *drive*, or are you? Is Karen going to come, too? ~~You~~ *Are you* going to bring food, or
> should we buy something there? And what *are* you going to do after the game? Do you
> want to come to our house?
>
> In your opinion, who ~~be~~ *is* going to win this year? I don't have any idea, but I know
> it's going ~~being~~ *to be* an exciting game. The Hurricanes really want to be champions this
> year. They ~~is~~ *are* going to play their best.
>
> > See you soon,
> >
> > George

7) Writing

Imagine that you and your friend Louis have made plans to go out on Saturday evening. You want to see a movie and eat in a new restaurant. On a separate sheet of paper, write a note to another friend, Marta. Tell Marta about your plans. Where are you going to eat? What film are you going to see? What are you going to do after the movie?

> Dear Marta,
>
>   Louis and I are planning to go out on Saturday evening.
> Do you want to come with us? First we're going to eat at
> the new Italian restaurant on Main Street. I heard it's
> very good . . . .

18 The Future with *Will*

FORM

1 **Examining Form**

Tim is talking with his mother, Margaret. Read the conversations and complete the tasks below.

> **Tim:** Mom, I'm going to Josh's house today after school.
>
> **Margaret:** All right. Are you going to be home for dinner?
>
> **Tim:** I don't know. <u>I'll call</u> you.
>
> **Margaret:** When are you going to do your homework?
>
> 5   **Tim:** Josh and I will work on it together. I promise.
>
> *Later on the phone . . .*
>
> **Tim:** Hi, Mom. We finished our homework and Josh's mother invited me for dinner here. Is that OK?
>
> **Margaret:** I guess so. What time are you going to be home?
>
> 10   **Tim:** It won't be late. We're going to have dinner in about half an hour. Then Josh and I want to watch something on TV, but I'll leave right after that. I'll be home before nine.
>
> **Margaret:** I won't be here. I'll be at your grandmother's. But that's OK. I'll see you when I get back.

1. Look at the underlined example of the affirmative form of the future with *will*. Underline five more examples. Does the form of *will* change with different subjects?

_____

2. Circle two examples of the negative form of *will*.

Working on the Future with *Will*

Complete the conversations with *will* or *won't*.

1. **A:** Are you going to be home for dinner?

   B: No, I __won't__. I have a meeting tonight.

2. **A:** I need help with my suitcase.

   B: Give it to me. I __will__ carry it.

3. **A:** Kathy __won't__ be at the party tomorrow.

   B: That's too bad. We __will't__ miss her.

4. **A:** Goodnight, Stan. See you on Monday.

   B: No, you __won't__. I __will__ be on vacation then.

5. **A:** __Will__ you meet me at the airport?

   B: Of course I __will__.

6. **A:** Who __will__ win the game?

   B: The Sox __will__.

MEANING AND USE

Making Predictions

Read the situations. Write one possible prediction with *will* and one with *won't* for each situation.

1. Bob hates fish. His mother is making fish for dinner tonight.

   He'll ask her to make something else. He won't eat it.

2. John and Sheila want to buy a new house. They don't have much money, and houses are expensive.

   They will save a lot of money. They won't buy a house for a long time.

3. Sue doesn't like her present job. She sees an advertisement for an interesting job in her field.

   She will apply for a new job. She won't stay at her present job for very long

4. Victor is working on a big project. His computer breaks down. New computers are very expensive.

   Victor will borrow a computer from a friend He won't buy a new one.

Read the situations. Choose a phrase from the box to make a promise for each situation. Use *will* or *won't*.

5 write it tomorrow	4 do the dishes in the morning
3 tell anyone	6 stay up late tonight
1 be there on time	2 water the plants this afternoon

1. You're going out on a date. Your date doesn't want you to be late. You say,

   I'll be there on time.

2. You're responsible for taking care of the garden at your house. Your parents remind you that garden is very dry. You say,

   I will water the plants this afternoot.

3. A friend tells you some gossip. She wants you to keep it a secret. You say,

   I won't tell any one.

4. You made a mess in the kitchen. Your roommate wants to know when you're going to clean it up. You say,

   I will do the dishes in the morning.

5. Your boss asked you to write a report. You were very busy this week and didn't do it. You say,

   I will write it tomorrow.

6. You have a cold. Your mother wants you to go to bed early. You say,

   I won't stay up late tonight.

Read the conversations below. Make a decision using *will* in each situation

1. **Waiter:** Are you ready for dessert?
   You: Yes. I'll have some apple pie.

2. **Your roommate:** That music is terrible.
   You: _____

3. **Sales clerk:** This jacket only comes in black or tan.
   You: Hmm. _____

4. **Your friend:** You know, it's Amy's birthday tomorrow.
   You: That's right! _____

5. **Your friend:** It's cold in here.
   You: _____

6. **Travel agent:** There is a flight at 6:30 and one at 10:00.
   You: _____

COMBINING FORM, MEANING, AND USE

Read the conversations. What is the meaning of *will* in each situation? Circle the correct answer.

1. **A:** Do you prefer coffee or tea?
   B: I'll have coffee.
   กำทำนาย   *ตัดสินใจที่รวดเร็ว*
   a. prediction *พยากรณ์*   **b.** promise   **c.** quick decision

2. **A:** You broke my watch!
   B: I'm sorry. I'll replace it.
   a. prediction   **b.** promise   **c.** quick decision

3. **A:** When do we get our grades?
   B: We'll probably get them on Thursday.
   a. prediction   **b.** promise   **c.** quick decision

4. **A:** Look at those clouds!
   B: It will probably rain tonight.
   a. prediction   **b.** promise   **c.** quick decision

5. **A:** Don't forget to call me.
   B: I won't.
   a. prediction   **b.** promise   **c.** quick decision

6. **A:** We have a seat on the flight at 3 o'clock.
   B: I'll take it!
   a. prediction   **b.** promise   **c.** quick decision

Imagine what the world will be like in five years. On a separate sheet of paper, write a paragraph about your predictions. Give reasons where possible.

> I think some things in the world will be better, and some will be worse. We will have more people because the population is growing quickly. However, there won't be as much pollution because . . . .

Chapters 17–18

A. Choose the word or phrase to complete each sentence.

1. What do you think? _____ tomorrow?
   a. Does it rain   **b.** Is it going to rain   **c.** Is it raining

2. I'm going to leave work early today because _____ a doctor's appointment.
   a. I'll have   **b.** I'm having   **c.** I have

3. Don't worry about your plants. _____ them while you're gone.
   a. I'll water   **b.** I'm watering   **c.** I water

4. Use our shampoo for a week and your hair _____ softer.
   a. going to feel   **b.** feels   **c.** will feel

5. My friends are going to go to a movie, but I'm _____.
   a. not go   **b.** not going   **c.** don't go

6. I'm sorry I made such a mess. _____ do it again.
   a. I'm not   **b.** I won't   **c.** I don't

7. We're hungry. When _____ ready?
   a. dinner is   **b.** dinner going to be   **c.** will dinner be

8. Mr. Jackson is 65. _____ retire soon.
   a. He probably   **b.** He'll probably   **c.** He's probably

B. Find and correct the errors in these sentences.

9. What are you going ^to do this afternoon?

10. Joe ~~will~~won't take a biology class.

11. The Tigers are, aren't ~~not~~ going to win the championship.

12. When are you going to ~~starting~~ start/from your new job?

13. ^am I not going to be in class tomorrow.

14. We'll ~~to~~ see you on Saturday.

15. What time ⌄we are going to have lunch?

16. Carol will ~~goes~~go to bed early tonight.

17. They are going ^not ~~not~~ to drive to Chicago.

C. Choose the best answer to complete each conversation.

18. **A:** Do you want tea or coffee?

   B: _____

   a. I have tea.

   b. I'll have tea.

   c. I had tea.

19. **A:** Who's going to win the game?

   B: I know our team _____.

   a. does

   b. are

   c. will

20. **A:** Can you keep a secret?

   B: Sure. _____

   a. You can.

   b. Where is it?

   c. I won't tell.

21. **A:** What are you going to do?

   B: _____

   a. No, we don't. Do you?

   b. We'll think of something.

   c. We will, thanks.

22. **A:** _____

   B: I know. Ted's going to be late.

   a. Did Ted come?

   b. The traffic is terrible.

   c. It was 7:30.

23. **A:** Everything will be all right.

   B: _____

   a. Yes, I do.

   b. Is he?

   c. I hope so.

24. **A:** How are you going home?

   B: _____

   a. I took the bus.

   b. I take the bus.

   c. I'll take the bus.

25. **A:** _____

   B: That's all right. I'll carry it.

   a. Your bag is really heavy.

   b. What are you carrying?

   c. Were those your bags?

19 *May* and *Might* for Present and Future Possibility

FORM

1 ▸ Examining Form

Julie sent this e-mail message to a friend who is studying at another college. Read the message and complete the tasks below.

To: Carol Swift
From: Julie Moon
Cc:
Subject: Summer plans

---

5 Hi Carol,

You asked me about my plans for the summer. Well, I'm not sure.
I'd really like to go backpacking in Europe. But my parents <u>might not</u>
(let) me. Also, I may not have enough money.
    What about a short trip in August? Maybe we could go to Mexico for a
10 week or two. How does that sound to you? Do you think that might work?
Let me know soon.

Julie

---

1. Underline all the examples of *may* and *might*. Circle the verbs that follow them. Look at the first example. Find two more.

2. Do *may* and *might* have different forms with different subjects? _____

3. What form of the verb follows *may* and *might*? _____

2 Writing Statements with *May* and *Might*

A. Rewrite these sentences. Use *may* or *may not*.

1. Maybe we'll go to Mexico.

   <u>We may go to Mexico.</u>

2. Maybe I'll be late tonight.

   _____

3. Maybe Jean won't be happy about the news.

   _____

4. Maybe I won't pass the course.

   _____

B. Rewrite these sentences. Use *might* or *might not*.

1. It's possible we'll have a test.

   <u>We might have a test.</u>

2. It's possible she'll take a trip soon.

   _____

3. It's possible we won't be home before 3:00.

   _____

4. It's possible they won't get married.

   _____

3 Working on *May* and *Might*

Complete the conversations with *may, may not, might,* or *might not.* More than one answer is possible.

1. **A:** I'll call you at home at 7:00 tonight.
   B: I <u>may not</u> be there then. Call me at 8:00.

2. **A:** What are you doing this weekend?
   B: I'm not sure. I _____ go camping with the kids.

3. **A:** Are the cookies ready yet?
   B: They _____ be. I'll check.

4. **A:** Are you going to the party alone?
   B: I _____ go with Sally.

MEANING AND USE

Understanding Possibility and Certainty

Choose the answer that expresses the meaning in parentheses.

1. **A:** Are you going to the party?

   B: _____ (certainty)

   a. I might.

   (b.) Yes, I am.

   c. I probably will.

2. **A:** What are you doing on Saturday?

   B: _____ (possibility)

   a. I'll work.

   b. I'm going to work.

   c. I may work.

3. **A:** Where's the car?

   B: _____ (certainty)

   a. Hmm. I'll look.

   b. It's in the garage.

   c. It might be on the street.

4. **A:** Who's that?

   B: _____ (possibility)

   a. It's going to be Paul.

   b. It's Paul.

   c. It might be Paul.

5. **A:** What are your plans for the summer?

   B: _____ (certainty)

   a. I'm going to take a class.

   b. I might take a class.

   c. Maybe I'll take a class.

6. **A:** Is Mary coming today?

   B: _____ (possibility)

   a. Yes, of course.

   b. She may not.

   c. No, she won't.

Writing About Possibility and Certainty

Read the situations. Write an affirmative or negative statement of possibility or certainty for each situation. Use *may, might, will,* or *be going to.* More than one answer is possible.

1. You go to school. The classroom door is locked.

   It may be a holiday today.

2. There is a party tonight. Sue wants to go, but she feels very tired.

   _____

3. It's Thursday, and you're at the gym. Dan often goes to the gym on Thursday.

   _____

4. Your train leaves at 3:00. It's 2:55. You are still waiting for a taxi at home.

   _____

5. Judy came home late. She's hungry, but there isn't any food in the kitchen.

   _____

COMBINING FORM, MEANING, AND USE

6 Understanding Meaning and Use

Choose the sentence that has the same meaning.

1. We may go to the park.
   - **a.** It's possible we'll go to the park.
   - **b.** We're going to go to the park.

2. We'll be at the office today.
   - **a.** We might be at the office.
   - **b.** We're going to be at the office.

3. The weather might be windy.
   - **a.** It will be windy.
   - **b.** Maybe it will be windy.

4. I won't make dinner.
   - **a.** I don't like to make dinner.
   - **b.** I'm not going to make dinner.

5. John might not agree with us.
   - **a.** It's certain he won't agree.
   - **b.** It's possible he won't agree.

6. The tickets may not be available.
   - **a.** Maybe there won't be any tickets.
   - **b.** We know there won't be any tickets.

7 Writing

A. Imagine that you are graduating from college this year. You are not sure yet what you will do. Use these questions to help you think about things you may or may not do.

- Will you get a job?
- Will you take a long vacation?
- Will you stay in school?
- Will you move to a new city?

B. On a separate sheet of paper, write a paragraph about your plans. Use affirmative and negative sentences with *may* and *might*.

> I'm graduating from college this year. I am not
> sure what I will do. I may travel to Europe with my
> my roommate. . . .

20 Can and Could for Present and Past Ability

FORM

1 Examining Form

A reporter from *Music World* is talking with Kathie Yoshimura, a famous violinist. Read the interview and complete the tasks below.

Music World: So, Kathie, you started playing the violin really early, right? Were you a child prodigy?

5 **Kathie:** I think I was. I started to practice the violin at about age two, and I could already play some Mozart pieces at age
10 three. And I learned how to play other instruments, too. For example, I could play the piano at five, and the cello at eight. I
15 couldn't play them very well right away, of course. I had to practice for a few years first.

Music World: Still, that's
20 amazing! Could you read music right away?

Kathie: Well, it's interesting. At first I learned to play without reading
25 music. I couldn't read music until age four.

Music World: Can you still play the piano and the cello?

30 **Kathie:** Yes, I can, but I play the violin much better.

1. Underline all the examples of *can* and *could*. Circle the verbs that follow them. Look at the first example. Find six more.

2. Look at the examples again. Find two negative verb forms with *could*. Write them with their subjects. _Couldn't play , couldn't read_

3. Find an example of a *Yes/No* question and a short answer with *can*.
   Can she play pino ?

Rewrite these sentences. Use the expressions in parentheses and make any necessary changes.

1. Bill can't play the piano. (a few years ago)

   Bill couldn't play the piano a few years ago.

2. Can you understand the lecture? (last night)

   Could you understand the lecture last night?

3. Teresa can't come to the party (last Sunday)

   Teresa couldn't come to the party last Sunday.

4. I can't finish the race. (last week)

   I couldn't finish the race. last week.

5. Hiro can speak three languages. (as a child)

   Hiro could speak three language. as a child.

6. I can't finish the test in one hour. (yesterday)

   I couldn't finish the test in one hour. yesterday.

7. Can you climb this mountain? (ten years ago)

   Could you climb this mountain? ten years ago?

8. Hanna can read very quickly. (at age six)

   Hanna could read very quickly. at age six.

3 **Completing Sentences about Present and Past Abilities**

Choose the correct modal to complete each sentence.

1. Last night I (can't /(couldn't)) sleep very well, so today I feel tired.

2. Fish (could /(can)) swim better than people.

3. I can read French, but I ((can't)/ couldn't) speak it.

4. Your answering machine wasn't working yesterday. I ((couldn't)/ can't) leave a message.

5. ((Can)/ Could) you play the guitar as a child?

6. I'm sorry, but I ((couldn't)/ can't) hear you. We have a bad connection.

7. Look! I ((can)/ could) type very quickly.

8. Greg ((couldn't)/ can't) help us move yesterday.

MEANING AND USE

4 Contrasting Past and Present Ability

Complete the paragraphs with *can, can't, could,* or *couldn't.*

A few years ago I wasn't very strong. I ___couldn't___ run and I
___couldn't___ exercise at a gym because I always got very tired. The only thing I
___could___ do was walk slowly. I wasn't happy because I ___couldn't___ play
tennis or go hiking with my friends. I ___couldn't___ live like that anymore.

So I decided to change my lifestyle. I walked a little each day. Now I
___can___ walk for several miles. I ___can't___ run very far but I'm
getting stronger every day. I ___can't___ lift weights and use many of the
machines at the gym. I ___can___ also go hiking with my friends. I still
___can't___ play tennis very well, but I am learning.

5 Writing About Results

Read the situations and complete a second sentence that talks about a result. Use *can,
can't, could* or *couldn't* and the phrases in the box. Make any necessary changes.

hear the telephone	buy some new toys
pay attention to the teacher	go for a walk
do the laundry	sing opera
get to work on time	go skiing

1. It's a beautiful day. We _can go for a walk._
2. It was very noisy at home last night. I _couldn't hear the telephone._
3. There's a lot of snow in the mountains. We _can go skiing._
4. Jack was very sleepy in class. He _couldn't pay attention to the teacher._
5. The children got money for their birthday. They _could buy some new toys._ (can / new)
6. Bryan has a beautiful voice. He _can sing opera._
7. The bus came late. I _can't get to work on time._ (couldn't)
8. I don't have any detergent. I _can't do the laundry._

COMBINING FORM, MEANING, AND USE

6) Editing

Some of the sentences in these conversations have errors. Find the errors and correct them.

1. **A:** I had some special abilities as a child. *ความสามารถ*

   B: Really? What ~~you~~ could you do?

   A: I could ~~to~~ play the piano and sing.

   B: Which ~~you~~ You could do better?

   A: I could sing better.

2. **A:** Can you ~~speaking~~ speak French?

   B: No, I ~~cann't~~ can't. Can you?

   A: Yes, and I can ~~to~~ speak a little German, too.

3. **A:** Can you You can cook?

   B: I can ~~to~~ cook a little.

   kind = type   **A:** What kinds of things you (can) cook?

   B: Oh, I can make simple dishes like spaghetti.

7) Writing

On a separate sheet of paper, write a paragraph about things you can do now that you couldn't do ten years ago, for example, speak English, drive, stay out late. Use *can*, *can't*, *could*, and *couldn't*.

> I can do many things now that I couldn't do ten years ago. I can speak four languages . . . .

21 Modals of Request and Permission

FORM

1 Examining Form

Wendy is going on a trip, and her friend Jennifer is taking care of her apartment. She leaves this note for Jennifer. Read the note and complete the tasks below.

> Jennifer,
>
> Thanks so much for taking care of my apartment this week.
> I know we talked about things, but here are some reminders.
> Would you please (feed) the cat twice a day? The cat food is
> 5 on the kitchen counter. Also, will you (check) her water bowl?
> She drinks a lot of water on hot days.
> The plants will probably be OK. But could you (check) them?
> Would you (do) me one more small favor? I receive lots of mail,
> and the mailbox can get very full. Would you (empty) the mailbox
> 10 every day? Please put the mail on the dining room table.
> By the way, have some of the chocolate cake in the
> refrigerator. It's delicious.
> Thanks again, and I'll see you next week.
>
> Wendy

1. Find the questions with the modals *could*, *will*, and *would*. Underline the modal and circle the main verb in each question. Look at the first example. Find five more.

2. What is the subject of each question? ___you___

2 Working on Short Answers with Modals

Choose the best answer for each conversation.

1. **A:** Could you help me?
   B: Sorry, I (~~can't~~ / won't) right now.

2. **A:** May I have some soup?
   B: Yes, you (will / ~~may~~).

3. **A:** Will you tell me the secret?
   B: No, I (may not / ~~won't~~)!

4. **A:** May I borrow your bike this afternoon?
   B: I'm sorry, you (~~can't~~ / can). I'm going biking with friends.

5. **A:** Would you please call Jack for me?
   B: Of course I (~~will~~ / would).

6. **A:** Can we use your lawnmower?
   B: No, you (won't / ~~cannot~~). It's broken.

3 Working on Questions with Modals

Write a question for each situation. Use the words in parentheses.

1. Your classmate has a pencil. You want to borrow it. (could)

   Could I borrow your pencil?

2. Your friend has a box of chocolates. You want one. (can)

   Can I have a chocolate?

3. You're carrying some heavy bags. You need some help. (would)

   Would you please help me? , Would you help me, please?

4. You're hot. You want your sister to open a window. (will)

   Will you open the window, please?

5. You're in your dorm room. You want your roommate to read your essay. (would)

   Would you read my essay?

6. You're in someone else's home. You would like to use the telephone. (may)

   May I use the telephone?

MEANING AND USE

4) Asking and Answering Questions

Match the questions on the left with the answers on the right.

_e_ 1. Would you please be quiet? I'm working.

_f_ 2. May I take this chair?

_a_ 3. Can I borrow your golf clubs?

_g_ 4. Could you translate this for me?

_h_ 5. Could I leave class early today?

_c_ 6. Will you take the kids to school today?

_b_ 7. Would you take a picture of us?

_d_ 8. May I use your pen?

a. Sure, you can. I don't need them.

b. Of course. What button do I press?

c. I can't. The car isn't working.

d. Sorry. It ran out of ink.

e. No problem. We'll talk later.

f. Sorry. Someone's sitting there.

g. I can. It will take me a few hours.

h. No, you can't. We have a test.

5) Contrasting Modals

Use words from the chart to write questions that match the meanings in parentheses.
More than one answer is possible.

May		borrow	now
Can	I	use	some tea
Could	you	leave	fruit
Will		do	your pen
Would			the laundry

1. (asking for permission)
   a. May I borrow some tea?   May I use your pen
   b. Can I use your pen?
   c. Could I leave now?

2. (making requests)
   a. Can I borrow some tea?
   b. May I do the laundry? (use, borrow)
   c. Can I borrow you pen
   Could you do the laundry?
   Will you leave now?
   Would you borrow some tea?
   Could you borrow the pen for me?

COMBINING FORM, MEANING, AND USE

6) Editing

Each conversation contains one error. Find the error and correct it.

1. **A:** Would you like ^to^ hear some jazz?

   B: Yes, I would. I love jazz.

2. *Can, would, could*
   A: ~~May~~ you take care of my house this weekend?   May you ✗

   B: Sorry, I can't.   May I ✓

3. *May, Can, Could*
   A: ~~Will~~ I use your umbrella?   No will, Would

   B: Of course. Go right ahead.

4. *Would, will*
   A: Could you please help me with the trash?

   B: Sorry, I w~~ou~~ldn't. I'm busy right now.   *Can't*

5. **A:** May I go to my room?

   B: No, you m~~ay~~n't. Finish your dinner first.   *may not, Can't*

6. **A:** Would you get some food for dinner?

   B: Of course. ~~I'd~~ get some after work.

   I'll, can

7) Writing

Imagine you are planning a surprise party for a friend or family member. On a separate sheet of paper, write an e-mail to four people who will help you plan the party. Make specific requests to each person in your e-mail. Ask one person for permission to have the party in his or her apartment.

To: Celia Getz
From: Lisa Miller
Cc: Elena Markov, Derek Milton, Juan Ruiz
Subject: John's Surprise Party

Hi Celia, Elena, Derek, and Juan,

I am so excited about the party, but I need a lot of help. Thanks for your help! Celia, could you please make your delicious chili and bring . . . .

---

22 Modals of Advice, Necessity, and Prohibition

FORM

1 Examining Form

Mike and Jeremy live in dormitories. They are talking about the rules they have to follow. Read the conversation and complete the tasks below.

> **Mike:** What is your dormitory like, Jeremy? I hear they have strict rules.
>
> **Jeremy:** Yes they do! All the residents <u>must</u> (do) certain things. We <u>have to</u> (take) out the trash every Tuesday and Thursday. We also <u>have to</u> (clean) the kitchen and bathroom.
>
> 5   **Mike:** Are there rules about hours? Do you <u>have to</u> (be) in your room by a certain time?
>
> **Jeremy:** Yeah we do. Last week I stayed out after 1:00 A.M., and the floor manager came to me and said, "You <u>shouldn't</u> (stay out) so late. You <u>must</u> (be) back in the dormitory by midnight."
>
> 10   **Mike:** Wow! My dorm is really different. I <u>don't have to</u> (clean). And I <u>don't have to</u> (be) in my room by midnight. No one checks on us.
>
> **Jeremy:** You're lucky!

1. Find all affirmative and negative examples of *must, should* and *have to*. Underline each modal and circle the verb that follows it. Look at the first example. Find seven more.

2. What verb form follows the modals? _____

3. Do modals change in form? _____

_____

2 Forming Negative Statements with *Have to*, *Must*, and *Should*

Change the positive statements into negative statements.

1. You must work all weekend.

   You must not work all weekend.

2. Holly has to study tonight.

   Holly doesn't has to study tonight.

3. You should pay attention to her advice.

   You shouldn't pay attention to her advice.

4. I have to take this class.

   I don't have to take this class.

5. You must come tonight.

   You must not come tonight.

6. We should call Rosa now.

   We shouldn't call Rosa now.

3 Asking Questions with *Should* and *Have to*

Use the words and phrases to write questions with *should* and *have to* for these conversations. Remember to add *do* or *does* where needed.

1. you / study / have to / tonight

   A: Do you have to study tonight?

   B: Yes, I do. I have a test tomorrow.

2. we / buy / a new car / should

   A: Should we buy a new car?

   B: No, we shouldn't. We don't need one.

3. get up / what time / you / tomorrow / have to

   A: What time do you have to get up tomorrow?

   B: I have to get up by 7:00.

4. I / make a decision / have to / now

   A: Do I have to make a decision now?

   B: Yes, you do. It's important.

5. should / what / do / now / I

   A: What should I do now?

   B: Just wait here.

MEANING AND USE

4 **Using Modals to Make Recommendations**

Read each situation and make a recommendation about what the people should do.
Use *should* or *should not*. More than one answer is possible.

1. **Situation:** Betty has a very bad cold, but she wants to go to class tomorrow.
   Recommendation: _Betty should stay home and go to bed._

2. **Situation:** Brian's roommate is very messy. Brian always cleans up their room, but it
   makes him angry. _Brian should tell roommate._
   Recommendation: _Brian shouldn't clean up after↓ roommate._ _his_

3. **Situation:** Doris is always late for work. Her boss told her that she has to come to
   work on time, or she will lose her job _Doris shouldn't late_
   Recommendation: _Doris should come to work on time_

4. **Situation:** Ken and Barbara want to get married, but they don't have jobs and they
   don't have any money.
   Recommendation: _They should fine a job._

5. **Situation:** John wants to lose weight, but he doesn't know what to do. _He should exercise._ _He should eat healthy food._
   Recommendation: _He should diet. He shouldn't eat a junk food, John shouldn't eat so much_

6. **Situation:** Dan has a big deadline at work tomorrow. It's 4:00 P.M. and he has a lot
   more work to do.
   Recommendation: _He should work late today. He should stay working._

5 **Thinking About Meaning and Use**

Rewrite these sentences. Use affirmative and negative forms of *should, must,* and *have
to* in the new sentences. In some examples, more than one answer is possible.

1. Is it necessary for me to take the test? _necessary ≠ should , necessary = have to, must_

   Do I have to take the test?

2. I <u>suggest</u> that you go to bed soon.

   You should go to bed soon.

3. It's <u>important</u> that we pay this bill by the end of the month. _- have to_

   We must pay this bill by the end of the month.

4. It's <u>against</u> the law to smoke on an airplane. _law, rule = must, must not_

   You must not smoke on an airplane.

5. It isn't <u>necessary</u> for you to buy me a present.

   You don't have to buy me a present.

COMBINING FORM, MEANING, AND USE

6 **Editing**

In the sentences below, parents are talking with their children. Some of the sentences contain errors. Find the errors and correct them.

1. You should ~~sharing~~ *share* your toys with your brother.

2. That isn't polite. You must not ~~to~~ talk like that.

3. Tomorrow is a holiday, so you ~~haven't~~ *don't have to* to go to bed early tonight.

4. Your room is a mess. You shouldn't ~~to~~ throw all your clothes on the floor.

5. You have come right home after school today. *to , must*

6. You ~~has~~ *have to* to get Tammy a present for her birthday.

7 **Writing**

Keiko is having problems in her English class. She needs to improve her reading and writing skills to pass a big test next month. What should she do? On a separate sheet of paper, write a letter to Keiko and give her some advice. Use *should, must,* and *have to* in your sentences.

Dear Keiko,

You should read newspapers in English and keep a writing journal . . . .

Chapters 19–22

A. Use the words and phrases to form questions. Add *do* or *does* when necessary.

1. your / book / may / math / I / borrow

   May I borrow your math book?

2. see / at the picnic / will / I / this weekend / you

   Will I see you at the picnic this weekend?

3. you / help / I / can

   (May) Can I help you?

4. to school / you / me / would / drive /

   Would you drive me to school? (please)

5. she / work late / (have to) / tonight

   Does she have to work late tonight?

6. take / we / our vacation / should / when / this year

   When should we take our vacation this year?

7. could / when / I / you / see

   When could (can, may) I see you?

8. early / get up / tomorrow / you / (have to)

   Do you have to get up early tomorrow?

B. Match these answers with the questions in A.

__2__ **9.** You might. I'm not sure I'll have time.

__4__ **10.** Of course. What time should I pick you up?

__6__ **11.** Let's go in August.

__1__ **12.** Sure. Here you are.

__5__ **13.** Yes. Unfortunately, she does.

__8__ **14.** Yes. I have an appointment at 8:00.

__7__ **15.** I'll be free tomorrow afternoon.

__3__ **16.** Yes. I'm looking for the shoe department.

C. Choose the correct word or phrase to complete each sentence.

17. It isn't very late. We _____ leave yet.

    a. wouldn't　　**b.** don't have to　　**c.** might not

18. _____ you answer the doorbell, please?

    a. Should　　**b.** May　　**c.** Could

19. _____ you mail this letter for me, please?

    a. Would _Request_　　**b.** do　　**c.** should

20. You _____ finish your application today. It's important.

    a. must　　**b.** would　　**c.** may

21. _____ I park the car in the driveway?

    a. Will　　**b.** Would = you　　**c.** May - I

22. I'm tired. _____ you take me home now?

    a. Would　　**b.** Should　　**c.** May

23. I'm not sure of Elaine's age. She _____ be 23 or 24.

    a. has to　　**b.** might → not sure　　**c.** will

24. My friends are waiting for me. I _____ go now.

    a. would　　**b.** have to (should)　　**c.** could

25. It's Susan's birthday today. _____ you take her this present?

    a. Will　　**b.** Do　　**c.** Should

23 Object Pronouns; Direct and Indirect Objects

receive the Verb action   *Tells us to or for whom*

FORM

1 Examining Form

Read the paragraph about Chinese New Year and complete the task below.

The Chinese New Year

New Year's Day is one of the most important Chinese holidays. Before the New Year, people buy special foods for their families. They also buy new clothes to wear on the holiday. Families clean their houses and throw out old things. On New Year's Eve, many people return to their family homes. They prepare a large meal for their relatives. The adult family members give small children "red envelopes" with small amounts of money. In the morning of New Year's Day, people light firecrackers and burn incense. Then they have a special breakfast. Traditionally, they go to a local temple and pray to their gods later in the day. They also visit relatives and friends.

Look back at the article and find the words listed in the first column of the chart. Are they direct or indirect objects? Check (✓) the correct column.

	LINE	DIRECT	INDIRECT
1. special foods	4	✓	
2. their families	4	✓	✓
3. their houses	7	✓	
4. a large meal	11	✓	
5. their relatives	11		✓
6. small children	13	✓	✓
7. red envelopes	13	✓	
8. relatives and friends	22	✓	

2 Working on Object Pronouns

Complete each sentence with the correct object pronoun.

1. The holiday was great. I enjoyed _____it_____ very much.

2. Doug and I are leaving now. Do you want to come with _____us_____ ?

3. These math problems are difficult. Do you understand _____them_____ ?

4. Janet is back from vacation. I saw _____her_____ yesterday.

5. Here's my telephone number. Please call _____me_____ tomorrow.

6. You don't know me, but I know _____you_____ .

7. There's my brother. Let's talk to _____him_____ .

8. Where's the dictionary? I can't find _____it_____ anywhere.

3 Making Statements with Direct and Indirect Objects

A. Use the words and phrases to write statements with direct and indirect objects.

1. gave / to the students / Mr. Jones / a geography test
   Mr. Jones gave a geography test to the students.

2. for my brother and me / a special meal / my mother / is preparing
   My mother is preparing a special meal for my brother and me.

3. explained / Keiko / to her American friends / the Japanese holiday
   Keiko explained the Japanese holiday to her American friend

4. her new dress / to Lee / Julie / showed
   Julie showed her new dress to Lee.

5. to Susie / for her birthday / Jack / a card / sent
   Jack sent a card to Susie for her birthday

B. Rewrite the sentences in part A. Change the indirect objects to pronouns. If possible, use the indirect object + direct object pattern.

1. Mr. Jones gave them a geography test.
2. My mother is preparing (us) a special meal. (for us)
3. Keiko explained her the Japanese holiday. to them
4. Julie showed (him) her new dress. (to him)
5. Jack sent her a card for her birthday

MEANING AND USE

4 Using Indirect Objects

Use indirect objects to complete these sentences in a logical way. Remember to use *to* or *for* when necessary.   *don't use to or for*

1. In China parents give _their children_ "red envelopes" on New Year's Day.

2. Many people send cards _to their mother_ on Mother's Day.

3. On the last day of class, students often give _their teacher_ a gift.

4. On Valentine's Day some people give _love onec_ cards or flowers.

5. On Thanksgiving Day many Americans cook a special meal _for their families_

6. Many people organize birthday parties _for their friend_

7. Remember to say "happy birthday" _to people_ on their birthday.   *their friend*

8. On Halloween people give _children_ candy.

5 Using Direct and Indirect Objects

Choose the correct answer to complete each conversation. In some cases, more than one answer is possible.

1. **A:** Do you still have your bike?
   B: No, I sold ____.
   a. it to Jeffrey
   b. Jeffrey it

2. **A:** What did you get Sam for his birthday?
   B: I got ____.
   a. him a sweater
   b. a sweater to him

3. **A:** Do you understand the article?
   B: No. Please explain ____.
   a. these words to me
   b. these words for me

4. **A:** What do you need from her?
   B: I want to say ____.
   a. something to her
   b. her something

5. **A:** Chris sent ____ yesterday.
   B: Oh, really? How is he?
   a. an e-mail to us
   b. us an e-mail

6. **A:** What do you do on Thanksgiving?
   B: I always cook ____.
   a. a big dinner for my family
   b. my family a big dinner

7. **A:** What's that?
   B: Someone sent ____.
   a. you a package
   b. you to a package

8. **A:** What is he doing?
   B: He's telling ____.
   a. us a joke
   b. a joke to us

COMBINING FORM, MEANING, AND USE

Choose the best question to complete each conversation.

1. A: _____

   B: He gave them to Lisa.

   a. Who gave the gifts?

   b. Who did he give the gifts to?

2. A: _____

   B: Yes, I miss them a lot.

   a. Who do you miss?

   b. Do you miss your friends?

3. A: _____

   B: I sent them yesterday.

   a. What did you send?

   b. When did you send the cookies?

4. A: _____

   B: We celebrate it in the traditional way.

   a. How do you celebrate New Year's?

   b. When do you celebrate New Year's?

5. A: _____

   B: I was telling them a story.

   a. Who was you telling a story?

   b. What were you telling the children?

6. A: _____

   B: Yes. I saved some for you.

   a. Is there any cake?

   b. What did you save?

7 Writing

On a separate sheet of paper, write about a recent holiday that you spent with your family or friends. Use the questions below to help you.

- What holiday did you celebrate?
- Who did you celebrate it with?
- What kind of holiday is it?
- Did you cook any special food?
- Did you buy cards or presents?
- Did you enjoy it? Why or why not?

> I celebrated Noruz with my family a week ago. Noruz is the Iranian New Year. We celebrated it in the traditional way. For example, ...

24 Infinitives and Gerunds After Verbs

FORM

Chris Jones is talking with a co-worker about a recent business trip. Read the conversation and complete the tasks below.

Rio de Janeiro, Brazil

Dan: How was your trip to Brazil, Chris?

Chris: It was OK. I'm glad I <u>agreed to go</u>. It was my first time there, and I (loved seeing) the country. I didn't do very much work, though.

Dan: It sounds like you <u>expected to do</u> more. What happened?

5 **Chris:** Well, I arrived in Rio the day before the Carnival holiday. I <u>needed to talk</u> to Luiz, the new Brazilian manager, but nobody was available. People in Brazil really (like celebrating) Carnival.

Dan: I don't blame them. So what did you do?

Chris: I <u>decided to celebrate</u> the holiday, too. I (enjoyed walking) around the
10 city. I really (liked seeing) all the famous sights.

Dan: But you <u>wanted to meet</u> Luiz. Did you finally <u>speak to him</u>?

Chris: Yes, but when we (started working,) I felt very tired from the holiday!

1. Look at the underlined example of a verb + infinitive. Underline four more examples.

2. Look at the circled example of a verb + gerund. Circle four more examples.

2 Contrasting Verbs + Infinitives and Verbs + Gerunds

Complete the sentences with the correct form of the verb in parentheses.

1. I enjoy _listening_ (listen) to classical music.

2. Nicole and her husband discussed _taking_ (take) a trip to Mexico.

3. My brother promised _to help_ (help) me clean the yard.

4. Where did you decide _to go_ (go) last night?

5. After you finish _doing_ (do) your homework, we can watch TV.

6. Helen isn't happy at work. She wants _to find_ (find) a new job.

7. I expect _to see_ (see) my friends at the game tomorrow.

8. Can you imagine _making_ (make) a speech in front of hundreds of people?

9. I dislike _walking_ (walk) alone at night.

10. Emily plans _to return_ (return) to England next summer.

3 Forming Sentences with Infinitives and Gerunds

Use the words and phrases to make sentences. Make all necessary changes.

1. discussed / we / go / next year / to Boston

   We discussed going to Boston next year.

2. take / I / business trips / dislike / long

   I dislike taking long business trips.

3. work / Dave / kept / all week / on the project

   Dave kept working on the project all week.

4. they / enjoy / the piano / play

   They enjoy playing the piano.

5. need / us / they / a direct answer / give

   They need to give us a direct answer.

6. she / plan / tomorrow / go shopping

   She plan to go shopping tomorrow

7. finish / hope / I / tomorrow / this assignment

   I hope to finish this assignment tomorrow.

8. avoided / all day / she / to me / talk

   She avoided talking to me all day.

MEANING AND USE

4 Describing Activities

Complete each sentence in a logical way. Use a gerund or infinitive to describe an activity. More than one answer may be possible.

1. I don't like _to study_ on weekends. or studing

2. Do you enjoy _eating_ ethnic foods?

3. We agreed _to take_ a taxi, but we couldn't find one.

4. It began _raning_ in the afternoon. or to rain

5. I love _to watch_ old movies. or watching.

6. Ken refuses _to study_ French. to learn, to speak, to listen to

7. They promised _to buy_ the tickets, but they didn't. to give

8. We decided _to take_ the children to the park. to leave

5 Rewriting Sentences

Rewrite each sentence using one of the verbs in the box. Do not change the meaning.

discuss	admit	keep
refuse	dislike	begin

1. Robert doesn't like to write essays.

   Robert dislikes writing essays.

2. Sue won't speak to George.

   Sue refuse to speak to George.

3. He often arrives late.

   He keeps arriving late.

4. We talked about taking an art class.

   We discussed taking an art class.

5. I started to understand the lecture.

   I began to understand the lecture (understanding)

6. The secretary said that he didn't lock the office.

   The secretary admitted to not locking the office.

COMBINING FORM, MEANING, AND USE

6) Understanding Meaning and Use

Read the statements below. Choose the sentence that best describes each situation.

1. Bob and Elaine decided to move.
   - **a.** They are going to move.
   - **b.** They couldn't move.

2. I hated cleaning the bathroom.
   - **a.** I cleaned it, but I didn't enjoy it.
   - **b.** I refused to clean it. • I didn't clean.

3. Sally avoided talking about her job.
   - **a.** She promised to talk about it.
   - **b.** She didn't talk about it.

4. We discussed looking for a new apartment.
   - **a.** We might look for one.
   - **b.** We already looked for one.

5. Sandra prefers to eat at home.
   - **a.** She needs to eat at home.
   - **b.** She likes to eat at home.

6. Carol imagined taking a trip to Europe.
   - **a.** She went, and she enjoyed the trip.
   - **b.** She thought about a trip to Europe.

7) Writing

On a separate sheet of paper, write two paragraphs about your preferences when you go on vacation. In the first paragraph, write about activities you enjoy or prefer doing. In the second paragraph, write about activities you don't enjoy. Use verbs with infinitives and gerunds to discuss your likes and dislikes.

When I go on vacation, I love to relax. I often like to go to the beach or go camping . . . .

On my vacations I don't like to be too busy. I hate to drive long distances. I also dislike . . . .

Chapters 23–24

A. Choose the correct word or phrase to complete each sentence. In some cases, there are two correct answers.

1. My brother told _____ yesterday.
   - **a.** me a funny story
   - **b.** a funny story to me
   - **c.** a funny story me

2. We avoid _____ downtown early in the morning.
   - **a.** to drive
   - **b.** driving
   - **c.** drive

3. Sue bought _____ at the mall.
   - **a.** a present her mother
   - **b.** her mother a present
   - **c.** a present for her mother

4. It's getting late. We should _____ now.
   - **a.** leave
   - **b.** leaving
   - **c.** to leave

5. Does Julia plan _____ a trip this summer?
   - **a.** take
   - **b.** taking
   - **c.** to take

6. I'm cooking _____ tonight.
   - **a.** David a special meal
   - **b.** a special meal for David
   - **c.** a special meal to David

7. What would you like _____ tomorrow?
   - **a.** do
   - **b.** to do
   - **c.** doing

8. Bill started _____ more in restaurants after he left home.
   - **a.** eat
   - **b.** eating
   - **c.** to eat

B. Find and correct the errors in these sentences.

9. Can you explain us the problem? *for, to* — Can you explain the problem to us

10. I dislike to do the laundry. *doing*

11. When you get home, please me write a letter.

12. Kate is finally learning speaking Spanish. *to*

13. Do you enjoy to play volleyball? *plaing*

14. Did she show you it? *thing it to*

15. George sent a postcard me. *to* *me*

C. Choose the best response to complete each conversation.

16. **A:** Did she come to the party?

    B: _____

    a. No, she is at the party.

    (b.) I expected her to come, but she didn't.

    c. She isn't there.

17. **A:** Did you go swimming?

    B: _____

    ~~a.~~ Yes. We went to the pool. *past*

    (b.) No thanks. I don't like to swim.

    c. Yes, I do.

18. **A:** What do you do in your free time?

    B: _____

    a. No, not usually.

    b. I don't like to do it.

    (c.) I enjoy painting.

19. **A:** Did you go to the game?

    B: _____

    a. Yes, I avoided going.

    b. No, I had to go.

    (c.) No, I decided not to go.

20. **A:** Did you show them your award?

    B: _____

    a. No, they did not win.

    (b.) Yes, I showed it to them.

    c. Yes, they showed it to me.

21. **A:** I like to play tennis.

    B: _____

    a. I don't like to, either.

    b. No, I keep doing it.

    (c.) I prefer to play golf.

22. **A:** How often do they cook you a meal?

    B: _____

    a. I didn't cook it.

    (b.) About once a week.

    c. At their house.

23. **A:** What do you hate doing?

    B: _____

    (a.) Well, I don't like to dance.

    b. Actually, I like it a lot.

    c. No, but I'd rather not.

24. **A:** Did they tell you the answer?

    B: _____

    a. No, you didn't tell it to me.

    b. No, I didn't tell it to them.

    (c.) No, they didn't tell it to us.

25. **A:** Are you a college student?

    B: _____

    a. Yes, I wanted to go, but I didn't.

    (b.) No, but I hope to start soon.

    c. Yes, I finished two years ago.

25 Comparatives

FORM

Examining Form

Read the conversations and complete the tasks below.

CONVERSATION 1

Carol: So who is <u>older</u>, Stefan or Tomek? They seem about the same age to me.

Linda: Hmm. Stefan is ~~taller~~ but I think he is a year or two <u>younger</u>.

Carol: Which one do you know (better)?

5 **Linda:** Stefan, I guess, <u>but I like them both</u>. Stefan is <u>more sociable</u>. Tomek seems (quieter,) but I think he's just shy.

ชอบสังคม

[handwritten margin notes:]
- older (T and St)
- taller (St)
- younger (St)
- more sociable (St)
- quieter (T)
- shoter (T)
- darker (hair)
- more attractive (Linda)
- prettier (Linda)
- more outgoing (Carol)

CONVERSATION 2

Stefan: Those girls are <u>really</u> nice. Which one is Linda? She's the <u>shorter</u> one, right?

Tomek: Right. She also has <u>darker</u> hair. Who do you think is <u>more</u>
10 <u>attractive</u>?

Stefan: Linda is <u>prettier</u>, maybe, but Carol is <u>more outgoing</u>.

Tomek: I agree. She dances (better,) too.

---

1. Look at the underlined example of the comparative form of an adjective. Underline nine more examples of comparative adjectives.

2. Look at the circled example of the comparative form of an adverb. Circle one more example of a comparative adverb.

A. Are the words below adjectives or adverbs? Write *ADJ* for adjectives and *ADV* for adverbs.

ADV 1. badly _more badly_

ADV 2. slowly _more slowly_

ADJ 3. interesting _more interessting_

ADJ 4. good _better_

ADJ 5. friendly _friendlier / more friendly_

ADJ 6. efficiently _more efficiently_

ADJ 7. slow _slower_

ADJ 8. useful _more useful_

ADV 9. cheaply _more cheaply_

ADJ 10. safe _safer_

ADJ 11. famous _more famous_

ADV 12. well _better_

B. Write the comparative form of the adjectives or adverbs in part A.

Complete each sentence with the comparative form of the word in parentheses.

1. Dan is a ___more reliable___ (reliable) worker than Bob.

2. Which snack is ___more healthy___ (healthy), fruit or candy? or _healthier_

3. Marcia plays the violin ___better___ (well) than her sister does.

4. You can do math problems ___more accurately___ (accurately) with a calculator.

5. It's ___cooler___ (cool) today than it was yesterday.

6. To me, swimming is ___more enjoyable___ (enjoyable) than running.

7. Texas is ___bigger___ (big) than California.

8. Derek acts ___more responsibly___ (responsibly) than his brother.

9. Linda drives ___faster___ (fast) than I do.

10. Careful! This box is ___heavier___ (heavy) that that one.

for close   _for far away_

MEANING AND USE

Comparing Two People

Look at the information in the chart. Write two sentences comparing George and Silvia.

	GEORGE	SILVIA
1.	isn't very popular	is very popular
2.	is a good student	isn't a good student
3.	is 19 years old	is 18 years old
4.	talks at an average speed	talks fast
5.	is very intelligent	is intelligent
6.	doesn't dance well	dances very well

1. *George is less popular than Silvia. Silvia is more popular than George.*
2. George is better student than Silvia. Silvia is worse than George
3. George is ~~more~~ older than Silvia. Silvia is ~~less~~ younger than George
4. George is talk less average speed. Silvia is talks faster than George
5. George is more intelligent than Silvia. Silvia is less intelligent than George
6. George is less dance than Silvia. Silvia is dancers better than Silvia

5 **Expressing Opinions**

Write your opinions about the people or things below. Use a comparative adjective or an adverb in each sentence.

1. artists/lawyers

   Artists are more interesting than lawyers.

2. a giraffe/a horse

   A giraffe's neck is longger than a horse

3. history/mathematics

   History is easier than mathematics.

4. tennis/golf

   Tennis is more ~~inter~~ exciting than golf.

COMBINING FORM, MEANING, AND USE

6 **Thinking About Meaning and Use**

Rewrite the sentences below as comparisons. Write two sentences to express the comparison.

1. I'm hungry, but Ben isn't.

   I'm hungrier than Ben. Ben is less hungry than me.

2. Susan sings well. Betty sings very well.

   Susan sing ~~better~~ less than Betty. Betty sings better than Susan.

3. The apples are cheap. The pears are expensive.

   The apples are ^less cheaper than pears. The pears are more expensive than apples.

4. My new apartment isn't very convenient. My old apartment was convenient.

   My new apartment is less convenient than my old apartment.

5. I felt bad yesterday, but today I feel OK.

   I felt ~~bad~~ worse yesterday than today.

6. Dana exercises sometimes, but Bob exercises frequently.

   Bob exercises more frequently than Dana.

7 **Writing**

On a separate sheet of paper, write a paragraph comparing two people you know well. For example, you could write about your parents, two friends, or two people at work. How are the people similar, and how are they different? Use the comparative forms of adverbs and adjectives to express your comparisons.

> My parents are both intelligent people, but they are different in other ways. My father is quieter than my mother. At first he seems less interesting. My mother is more sociable. She talks faster . . . .

26 Superlatives

FORM

1 Examining Form

Hanna and Pete are talking about languages. Read the conversation and complete the tasks below.

> **Hanna:** How many languages do you know, Pete?
>
> **Pete:** Well, Danish is my native language, and I speak English, German, and some French.
>
> **Hanna:** That makes four. What language do you speak (the most fluently)?
>
> 5 **Pete:** My most fluent language is probably English, since I speak it <u>more frequently</u> than I speak Danish now.
>
> **Hanna:** What about German and French?
>
> **Pete:** I speak German better than French, but I want to improve my French. I think it's the most beautiful language in the world. What about you,
>
> 10 Hanna? What languages do you know?
>
> **Hanna:** I speak Korean and English, but I also know a little French. My Korean is the best. I once took some Spanish lessons, but I was the worst student in the class.

1. Look at the underlined example of the comparative in the conversation. Underline one more.

2. Look at the circled example of the superlative. Circle four more.

3. Which of the superlatives are adjectives? Which are adverbs?

_____

_____

2) Writing Adjective and Adverb Forms

Complete the chart below.

ADJECTIVE/ADVERB	COMPARATIVE	SUPERLATIVE
1. fluent	more fluent	the most fluent
2.	easier	
3. good		
4.	higher	
5.		the worst
6. expensive		
7.	more carefully	
8. small		
9.		the most interesting
10.	more slowly	

3) Using Superlative Adjectives and Adverbs

Complete each sentence with the superlative form of the word in parentheses.

1. Marcus is _____the tallest_____ (tall) boy in our neighborhood.

2. Tom, Paulo, and Dave work fast, but Rob works _____ (efficiently).

3. English is _____ (common) second language in many countries.

4. Who is _____ (good) student in the class?

5. Berlin is _____ (large) city in Germany.

6. Don't go to Joe's Diner. It's _____ (bad) restaurant in town.

7. Everyone in my family speaks French, but my sister speaks it

   _____ (fluently).

8. Sit in that chair. It's _____ (comfortable).

9. I love this painting by Monet. I think it's _____ (beautiful)

   picture in the museum.

10. Everyone in Diego's family speaks some Spanish, but her mother speaks

    it _____ (well).

MEANING AND USE

4   **Using Comparatives and Superlatives**

Complete the conversations with the appropriate comparative or the superlative forms of the words in the boxes. In some cases, more than one answer may be possible.

Conversation 1

high/good/intelligent/hard

A: Who got ___the highest___ grade on the last test?
                         1

B: Dave did. He usually gets _____ grades.
                                     2

A: Do you think he's _____ student in the class?
                           3

B: I don't know. But he certainly studies _____.
                                            4

Conversation 2

cheap/good

A: That meal was great. And it was _____ than dinner last night
                                           1
at Philippe's.

B: Yes, but I still think the food at Philippe's is _____ in town.
                                                   2

5   **Expressing Opinions**

Write your opinions about the following people or things. Use a superlative in each sentence, and use *least* in one or more examples.

1. expensive hobbies

   In my country, golf is the most expensive hobby.

2. beautiful movie actresses

   _____

3. good restaurants in my city or town

   _____

4. cheap ways to travel

   _____

5. efficient ways to learn a language

   _____

COMBINING FORM, MEANING, AND USE

6) Editing

Some of these sentences have errors. Find the errors and correct them.

1. I like Dr. Ross's class. It's ~~more~~ *the most* interesting class I'm taking this semester.

2. I don't understand you. Please speak more clearly.

3. My neighbors' apartment is very large. It's the largest apartment than the building.

4. Yuji drives the most fastly of all my friends.

5. Russian grammar is the most difficult than Italian grammar.

6. Min-woo's job starts at 7:00 A.M., so he gets up the earliest in his family.

7. The Nile is the longer river in the world.

8. Rick's a terrible tennis player. He plays the baddest of anyone I know.

7) Writing

On a separate sheet of paper, write a paragraph about the most interesting or most unusual person you know. It could be a friend, a relative, or someone in your imagination. Who is the person? In what way is he or she interesting or unusual? Use comparatives and superlatives to explain why this person is unique.

> My friend Sasha is the most unusual person I know.
> He is a better student than I am, and he has the most
> interesting hobbies of any of my friends . . . .

Chapters 25–26

A. Complete the conversations. Use the comparative or superlative form of the words in parentheses.

Conversation 1

A: How old is Megan? Is she your __older than__ (old) child?
1

B: No, she's in the middle. She's __younger__ (young) than Timothy but
2
__older__ (old) than Pete.
3

Conversation 2

A: Who's __better__ (good) teacher in your school?
4

B: Well, Mr. Chang is __more popular__ (popular), but I think Ms. Adams
5
works __harder__ (hard) than any other teacher.
6

Conversation 3

A: Is San Francisco __larger__ (large) than Los Angeles?
7

B: No, it's much __smaller__ (small), but it's also
8
__pretter__ (pretty). Some people say it's __more beautiful__ (beautiful)
9   10
city in the United States.

B. Find and correct the errors in these sentences.

11. Yesterday was ~~more~~ hot **hotter** than today.

12. I think Mexican food is a most delicious.

13. Is Chinese harder to learn from German?

14. Janice is the better writer in the class.

15. Dana runs the faster than Mike.

16. There are few monolingual people in Denmark than in England.

17. Who is the baddest player on the team?

18. Kim speaks the most slowest.

19. A kilo weighs the more than a pound.

C. Choose the best answer to complete each conversation.

20. **A:** Was the test difficult?

    B: _____

    a. No, it was harder.

    b. Yes, it was the easiest.

    c. It was easier than the last one.

21. **A:** How tall is your brother?

    B: _____

    a. That's true. He's taller.

    b. He's shorter than me.

    c. No, he isn't. He's short.

22. **A:** New York is the most exciting city in the U.S.

    B: _____

    a. It's also very expensive.

    b. Wasn't it?

    c. Why isn't it more exciting?

23. **A:** Carl is richer than us.

    B: _____

    a. But is he happier?

    b. Who's the richest?

    c. Do you make more money?

24. **A:** Is Tom more popular than Bill?

    B: _____

    a. Yes, Bill's the most popular.

    b. Yes, and he's better looking.

    c. Yes, Tom likes him a lot.

25. **A:** My grades are getting worse.

    B: _____

    a. You're right. They're much better.

    b. Don't worry. They're worse than mine.

    c. So what are you going to do about it?

Answer Key

Chapter 1 Simple Present Statements with *Be*

Exercise 1 (p. 1)

1. line 3: is
   line 4: is
   line 6: 's
   line 9: are
   line 11: are
   line 12: 're
   line 14: is
   line 14: 'm
   line 16: 's
   line 17: 'm
   line 18: 'm

2. line 12: aren't
   line 19: 'm not

3. line 12: They're
   lines 14, 17, 18: I'm
   line 6: isn't

Exercise 2 (p. 2)

2. Computervilla is a new company.
3. Bill is a new employee.
4. We are not students.
5. Kelly is in a sales meeting.
6. They are not in the office.

Exercise 3 (p. 2)

2. They're new employees.
3. It's not in Japan.
4. They're new.
5. She's not the president. OR She isn't the president.
6. We're teachers.
7. You're at work.

Exercise 4 (p. 3)

2. a programmer
3. old
4. from Brazil
5. at home
6. hot

Exercise 5 (p. 3)

2. a
3. a
4. a

5. b
6. b

Exercise 6 (p. 4)

2. Irina be Russian. *is*
3. He not is in my class.
4. Correct.
5. Correct.
6. They is from Japan. *are*
7. Correct.
8. It are hot and humid. *is*

Exercise 7 (p. 4)

Answers will vary.

Chapter 2 Questions with *Be*

Exercise 1 (p. 5)

1. line 7: What's his favorite kind of music?
   line 12: Where are you from?

2. line 5: Is he a business major, too?
   line 9: Are you a new student?
   line 12: Are you from Japan?

Exercise 2 (p. 6)

2. Is Diego from Mexico?
3. Am I late?
4. Are you and Jack students?
5. Are we ready?
6. Is Veronica busy?
7. Is it beautiful?
6. Are they lawyers?

Exercise 3 (p. 6)

2. Where is your office?
3. When is the meeting?
4. Who are your friends?
5. How is your boss?
6. What's on your desk?
7. Where are we?
8. How is the weather?
9. When is the wedding?
10. What is your name?

Exercise 4 (p. 7)

2. j
3. e
4. g
5. i
6. b
7. f
8. a
9. d
10. h

Exercise 5 (p. 7)

2. Where are Amy and Donna?
3. How is Paris?
4. Who is Donna?
5. Where is she from?
6. What is Donna?
7. How is the weather?
8. When is her flight?

Exercise 6 (p. 8)

    Brad: Hi. Are you a student here?

Marcus: Yes, I'm. I'm a freshman. *(I am)*

    Brad: What your name? *(is)*

Marcus: My name Marcus. *(is)*

    Brad: I'm Brad. Where are from, Marcus? *(you)*

Marcus: I from Beaver Falls. *(am)*

    Brad: ~~That is~~ near here? *(Is that)*

Marcus: No, it's a small town near Portland, Oregon.

    Brad: What your major (is)?

Marcus: Chemistry.

    Brad: Really? Chemistry ~~it's~~ my major, too! *(is)*

Exercise 7 (p. 8)

Answers will vary.

Chapter 3 Imperatives

Exercise 1 (p. 9)

1. line 2:   Paint
   line 3:   wait
   line 3:   Finish
   line 4:   Clean
   line 7:   Take
   line 9:   take
   line 10: Go
   line 11: turn
   line 14: Keep away

2. line 12: Do not eat
   line 12: Do not swallow
   line 13: Do not put

3. *do not* or *don't* + base form of verb

Exercise 2 (p. 10)

2. Turn
3. Don't talk
4. Look
5. close
6. Don't leave
7. Listen
8. Get

Exercise 3 (p. 10)

Answers will vary. Some examples are:

2. Walk down Maple Street. Turn left on 1st Street and walk straight. The supermarket is on the corner of 1st Street and Jones Avenue.
3. Walk straight on Maple Street. Cross 1st Street. The library is on your left.
4. Walk down Maple Street. Turn left on Oak Street and turn right on Jones Avenue.

Exercise 4 (p. 11)

2. b
3. d
4. a
5. c
6. a

Exercise 5 (p. 11)

2. a
3. b
4. b
5. a
6. b

Exercise 6 (p. 12)

2. Correct.
3. ~~Eat~~ in class. *(Don't eat)*
4. Correct.
5. Don't ~~be~~ on time for class. *(B)*
6. Don't ~~ask~~ questions. *(A)*
7. ~~Leave~~ your homework at home *(Don't leave)*
8. Don't ~~be~~ polite to the teacher. *(B)*

Exercise 7 (p. 12)

Answers will vary.

See page 143 for Key to Review: Chapters 1–3.

Chapter 4 Introduction to Nouns

Exercise 1 (p. 15)

1. line 2:   place
   line 4:   living room
   line 5:   fireplace
   line 5:   neighborhood

line 7: apartment
line 10: building
line 10: problem

2. line 10: neighbors
line 11: men
line 11: musicians

Exercise 2 (p. 16)

2. Johnsons
3. A studio
4. women
5. Cars
6. country
7. boxes
8. a tenant OR tenants
9. people
10. a student

Exercise 3 (p. 16)

PLURAL FORM	/s/	/z/	/ɪz/
2. watches			✓
3. sodas		✓	
4. maps	✓		
5. dorms		✓	
6. books	✓		
7. hotels		✓	
8. offices			✓
9. computers		✓	
10. leaders		✓	
11. minutes	✓		
12. wishes			✓

Exercise 4 (p. 17)

2. f, g
3. a, b, c
4. d, h

Exercise 5 (p. 17)

2. a hill
3. neighbors
4. a window
5. an hour
6. work

Exercise 6 (p. 18)

We had a great time̶s̶ in Florida. How are you? And how
are your c̶h̶i̶l̶d̶s̶ _children_ ? Are you happy with your new house?
How i̶s̶ _are_ your neighbors there?

I am happy at my new job. My boss̶e̶s̶ is great. The other
employee _s_ are nice, too. Call me tomorrow evening̶s̶. I'm
at ̶a̶ home after 7:00.

Exercise 7 (p. 18)
Answers will vary.

Chapter 5 Introduction to Count and Noncount Nouns

Exercise 1 (p. 19)

1. line 4: detergent
line 4: bottle
line 5: garbage
line 5: can
line 6: can
line 7: coffee
line 7: tea
line 8: food
line 8: food
line 8: refrigerator
line 9: kitchen
line 10: electricity

2. **Count Nouns**

line 1: kitchen
line 4: bottle
line 5: can
line 6: can
line 8: refrigerator
line 9: kitchen

   Noncount Nouns

line 4: detergent
line 5: garbage
line 7: coffee
line 7: tea
line 8: food
line 8: food
line 10: electricity

3. line 2: dishes
line 2: utensils
line 2: shelves
line 3: shelves
line 5: bottles
line 6: cans
line 7: cans
line 7: guests
line 10: lights

Exercise 2 (p. 20)

2. C
3. C
4. N
5. N
6. C

Exercise 3 (p. 20)

A. 2. is
3. are
4. is
5. is
6. is

B. 2. a
   3. a
   4. a
   5. b
   6. b

Exercise 4 (p. 21)

2. paper
3. are
4. Coffee
5. is
6. cans
7. flour
8. is
9. water
10. glass

Exercise 5 (p. 21)

2. Knowledge
3. a bike
4. Mathematics
5. weather
6. an apple
7. Litter
8. water
9. a cup
10. a friend

Exercise 6 (p. 22)

2. b
3. b
4. a
5. a
6. b

Exercise 7 (p. 22)

Answers will vary.

See page 143 for Key to Review: Chapters 4–5.

Chapter 6 Descriptive Adjectives

Exercise 1 (p. 25)

1. line 2: expensive
   line 3: old
   line 3: French
   line 5: black
   line 5: nice
   line 5: large
   line 9: oval
   line 10: perfect
   line 13: expensive

2. line 2: nice
   line 2: expensive
   line 5: nice
   line 5: large
   line 10: perfect
   line 13: expensive

3. line 3: old
   line 3: French
   line 5: black
   line 9: oval

Exercise 2 (p. 26)

2. The clothes are cheap.
3. Look at the green dress!
4. The old videos are from the 1950s.
5. How much is the wool jacket?
6. They're beautiful shoes.
7. Is the gold jewelry for sale?
8. Holly is tired and hot.
9. Don't buy the broken TV.
10. The clothing is expensive.

Exercise 3 (p. 26)

2. Meet my little sister.
3. Don't buy an expensive coat.
4. It's a birthday present.
5. Belgium is a small country.
6. Look at my new shoes.
7. The diamond ring is from my grandmother.
8. Try the Italian restaurant on Main Street.

Exercise 4 (p. 27)

2. small
3. round
4. Brazilian
5. delicious
6. rainy

Exercise 5 (p. 27)

2. chocolate
3. kitchen
4. school
5. gold
6. Cotton
7. phone
8. chicken

Exercise 6 (p. 28)

2. h
3. a
4. d
5. c
6. g
7. b
8. e

Exercise 7 (p. 28)

Answers will vary.

Chapter 7 Possessives and Demonstratives

Exercise 1 (p. 29)

1. line 9: wife's
   line 10: children's
2. line 5: that's
3. line 2: Mine
   line 4: his

Exercise 2 (p. 30)

2. A: Whose uncle is Mr. Sanborn?
   B: Barry and John's.
3. A: Whose house is next door?
   B: The Joneses'.
4. A: Whose books are on the desk?
   B: My kids'.
5. A: Whose lunch is on the table?
   B: Jonathan's.
6. A: Whose gray cat is under the desk?
   B: The manager's.

Exercise 3 (p. 30)

1. These
2. Who's, That's
3. this, it's
4. your, They're
5. This, Its
6. sister's, mine

Exercise 4 (p. 31)

2. Their
3. Mine
4. Her
5. Its
6. His
7. yours
8. our

Exercise 5 (p. 31)

B. 2. a
3. a
4. b
5. b
6. a

Exercise 6 (p. 32)

2. A: Are ~~that~~ those books old?

   B: Yes, they're very old.

3. A: Is this your shirt?

   B: Yes, it's ~~my~~ mine.

4. A: Whose pictures are they?

   B: ~~Their~~ They're Mr. Stewart's.

5. A: What's your ~~fathers'~~ father's first name?

   B: It's Harry.

6. A: Is that car Judy's?

   B: No, it's her~~s~~ brother's.

Exercise 7 (p. 32)

Answers will vary.

See page 143 for Key to Review: Chapters 6–7.

Chapter 8 The Present Continuous

Exercise 1 (p. 35)

1. line 6: are . . . doing
   line 7: are . . . going
   line 7: are . . . taking
   line 8: is . . . taking
   line 10: 'm . . . not wearing
   line 11: 'm wearing
   line 11: is calling
   line 12: 's asking

2. a. line 8: Is he still taking acting lessons?
   b. line 6: How are you doing this semester?
      line 7: And how are your classes going?
      line 7: . . . are you taking three or four classes?
   c. line 10: I'm still not wearing my fall clothes.

Exercise 2 (p. 36)

2. am making
3. are the kids doing
4. is studying
5. is watching
6. Is it still snowing
7. are you doing
8. am relaxing
9. Are you enjoying
10. am working
11. am enjoying
12. are thinking

Exercise 3 (p. 36)

2. Are you drinking coffee?
3. What is Margaret doing these days?
4. Am I making too much noise?
5. How is it going?
6. Are they leaving now?
7. Are you thinking about me?
8. Is Luisa playing computer games?

Exercise 4 (p. 37)

Answers will vary. Some examples are:
2. It's raining. The sun isn't shining.
3. We aren't dieting. We're eating a big breakfast.
4. David and Edna aren't dancing. They're reading.
5. I'm brushing my teeth. I'm not brushing my hair.
6. Lori isn't swimming. She's playing tennis.

Exercise 5 (p. 37)

2. —
3. MS
4. —
5. —
6. MS

Exercise 6 (p. 38)

2. a
3. b
4. a
5. b
6. a

Exercise 7 (p. 38)

Answers will vary.

Chapter 9   The Simple Present

Exercise 1 (p. 39)

1. line 2:   sounds
   line 3:   means
   line 4:   have
   line 6:   see
   line 7:   work
   line 8:   take
   line 11: teach
   line 12: write
   line 13: 's
   line 14: don't have
   line 14: write

   The speakers use the simple present tense.

2. line 14: No, I don't have much time during the week.
   do + not (or *don't*) + base form of the verb

Exercise 2 (p. 40)

A. 2. He doesn't get up before 9:00 A.M.
   3. He doesn't have a job.
   4. Alex swims at the pool every morning.
   5. Alex does not play a musical instrument.
   6. His friends live near him.
   7. They visit him on weekends.
   8. Alex studies on Sunday night.

B. 2. She gets up before 9:00 A.M.
   3. She has a job.
   4. Lisa doesn't swim at the pool every morning.
   5. Lisa plays a musical instrument.
   6. Her friends don't live near her.
   7. They don't visit her on weekends.
   8. Lisa doesn't study on Sunday night.

Exercise 3 (p. 41)

2. weighs
3. hurts
4. Do . . . smell

5. don't understand
6. own
7. doesn't cost
8. taste
9. belongs
10. love

Exercise 4 (p. 41)

2. c
3. d
4. h
5. a
6. g
7. b
8. f

Exercise 5 (p. 42)

Student: I study math, chemistry, and history.

Reporter: Do you ~~taking~~ *take* classes every day?

Student: No, I ~~do~~ take classes four days a week.

Reporter: How many hours a day ~~are~~ *do* you study?

Student: I ~~studying~~ *study* about three hours every day.

Reporter: Where your family (does) live?
        live

Student: They ~~lives~~ *live* in Japan.

Reporter Do you ~~visiting~~ *visit* them often?

Student: No, I ~~doesn't~~ *don't*. I ~~sees~~ *see* them about once a year.

Exercise 6 (p. 42)

Answer will vary.

Chapter 10   Adverbs of Frequency

Exercise 1 (p. 43)

1. line 5:   rarely
   line 7:   never
   line 10: sometimes
   line 10: generally
   line 12: often
   line 13: not very often
   line 13: almost always

2. line 5: usually

3. usually, generally

Exercise 2 (p. 44)

2. Joan often works around the house.
3. Bob rarely works around the house.
4. Bob and Joan rarely get up early.
5. Bob usually plays tennis.
6. Joan never plays tennis.

Exercise 3 (p. 44)

2. He doesn't usually work late.
3. I miss my family sometimes. OR I sometimes miss my family. OR Sometimes I miss my family.
4. He rarely goes out.

5. How often do you drink milk?
6. I never eat chocolate.
7. Are you lonely sometimes? OR Are you sometimes lonely?
8. When do you usually eat dinner?

Exercise 4 (p. 45)
Answers will vary. Some examples are:
2. Alan always talks on his cell phone.
3. My brothers never eat any vegetables.
4. I almost never pay bills on time.
5. Dana rarely eats breakfast.
6. Diego and I usually stay up late.

Exercise 5 (p. 45)
Answers will vary. Some examples are:
2. She is often at home on weekends.
3. Brad always eats out.
4. Kim rarely drinks coffee.
5. Karen never calls me.
6. We are almost always late.

Exercise 6 (p. 46)
Answers will vary. Some examples are:

I am a delivery person. I <u>always</u> work four days a week. I <u>often</u> work Monday through Thursday. However, <u>sometimes</u> I work Tuesday through Saturday. I <u>rarely</u> get overtime. In the evening, I am <u>generally</u> at home with my wife and children. <u>Occasionally</u>, I go out alone to visit friends. Those nights I <u>never</u> stay out late. I like to be in bed before midnight.

Exercise 7 (p. 46)
Answers will vary.

See page 143 for Key to Review: Chapters 8–10.

Chapter 11 The Simple Past of *Be*

Exercise 1 (p. 49)
1. line 2:   was
    line 2:   were
    line 3:   was
    line 3:   Was
    line 5:   wasn't
    line 6:   were
    line 6:   were
    line 7:   weren't
    line 8:   were
    line 8:   were
    line 9:   was
    line 10: wasn't
    line 10: was
    line 10: wasn't

2. a. line 2:   It was nice.
        line 2:   We were lucky.
        line 3:   . . . the weather was beautiful.
        line 6:   We were over at your house . . . .
        line 8:   We were at the movies.
        line 10: The story was silly . . . .
    b. line 7:   . . . you weren't there.
        line 10: It wasn't great.
        line 10: . . . the acting wasn't very good.
    c. line 3:   Was it busy at the office?
    d. line 5:   No, it wasn't.
    e. line 6:   Where were you last night?
        line 8:   What time were you there?
        line 9:   So, how was the movie?
    f. line 8:   We were at the movies.
        line 9:   Around 8:30.
        line 10: It wasn't great.

Exercise 2 (p. 50)
2. was
3. were
4. were
5. were
6. was

Exercise 3 (p. 50)
2. Where were Daniel's parents born?
3. Was Mozart a philosopher?
4. What was the play like?
5. When were you and your wife in London?
6. Who was that?

Exercise 4 (p. 51)
2. f
3. e
4. c
5. a
6. b

Exercise 5 (p. 51)
A. 2. Were you a happy child?
   3. Where were you three years ago?
   4. Were you sick last week?
   5. Was your hair short last year?
   6. Who was your last English teacher?
   7. Were you a student last year?
   8. Who was your best friend in grade school?

B. Answers will vary.

Exercise 6 (p. 52)
2. was a waiter
3. was comfortable
4. was cloudy
5. Were . . . in school
6. were delicious

Exercise 7 (p. 52)

Answers will vary.

Chapter 12 The Simple Past

Exercise 1 (p. 53)

1. **Regular**
   line 11: decided
   line 18: passed
   line 20: used
   line 26: curled
   line 26: called
   line 28: looked

   Irregular
   line 13: wore
   line 14: were
   line 23: were
   line 24: grew
   line 25: grew
   line 32: wore
   line 33: became
   line 37: grew
   line 37: grew
   line 39: came back

2. line 16: were not
   line 21: didn't grow
   line 38: didn't shave

Exercise 2 (p. 54)

A.

SIMPLE PAST FORM	/d/	/t/	/ɪd/
wanted			✓
used	✓		
invented			✓
called	✓		
watched		✓	

B.

2. came
3. drove
4. found
5. went
6. heard
7. met
8. saw
9. spoke
10. taught
11. thought
12. won

Exercise 3 (p. 54)

2. They did not wear beards or mustaches.
3. Napoleon Bonaparte had hundreds of gloves.
4. Victorian women did not show their legs.

5. Working class men did not wear suits and top hats.
6. Beards became fashionable again in the late 1960s.

Exercise 4 (p. 55)

2. b
3. a
4. f
5. e
6. c

Exercise 5 (p. 55)

Conversation 1
2. didn't feel
3. stayed
4. Did . . . call
5. went
6. got

Conversation 2
1. was
2. enjoyed
3. Did . . . do
4. rented
5. saw
6. ate

Exercise 6 (p. 56)

A. 2. moved
3. went
4. met
5. married
6. wrote
7. started
8. died

B. Answers will vary. Some examples are:
2. He moved to Missouri.
3. Where did he go with his brother?
4. Who did he meet in San Francisco?
5. He married her in 1870.
6. Did he write *The Adventures of Huckleberry Finn* in 1870?
7. What did he do in 1884?
8. He died in 1910.

Exercise 7 (p. 56)

Answers will vary.

Chapter 13 The Past Continuous

Exercise 1 (p. 57)

1. line 4:   was taking
   line 5:   (was) singing
   line 6:   was . . . making
   line 10: was making
   line 11: were sitting
   line 16: was going
   line 16: was listening
   line 19: was driving
   line 21: was . . . sleeping
   line 23: was . . . moving

2. The two forms are *were* and *was* + base form of verb + *ing*.

3. I didn't notice anything because I was driving.

Exercise 2 (p. 58)

Answers will vary. Some examples are:
2. was reading a book.
3. wasn't watching TV.
4. weren't playing a video game.

Exercise 3 (p. 58)

2. Rick was riding in an elevator.
3. My brother and I were driving to the beach.
4. The airplane passengers were having dinner.

Exercise 4 (p. 59)

2. was blowing
3. were sitting
4. were watching
5. were sleeping
6. heard
7. got up
8. looked
9. saw
10. hit
11. was
12. fell

Exercise 5 (p. 59)

Conversation 1
2. called
3. were you doing
4. was watching

Conversation 2
1. saw
2. didn't see
3. Were . . . going
4. was shopping

Exercise 6 (p. 60)

It ~~is~~ *was* sailing from Southampton to New York City. Over 2,200 people were ~~traveled~~ *traveling* on the ship. Many of the passengers ~~slept~~ *were sleeping* in their cabins. The ship ~~were~~ *was* going too fast in dangerous waters. The crew ~~wasn't seeing~~ *didn't see* the iceberg. The ship hit an iceberg. The *Titanic* ~~was sinking~~ *sank* to the bottom of the ocean.

Exercise 7 (p. 60)

Answers will vary.

See page 144 for Key to Review: Chapters 11–13.

Chapter 14 Articles

Exercise 1 (p. 63)

1. line 4:   an
   line 8:   an
   line 8:   a
   line 10: a
   line 14: a
   line 14: a

   We use *a* before nouns that start with a consonant sound. We use *an* before nouns that start with a vowel sound.

2. line 9:   The
   line 10: the
   line 10: the
   line 12: the
   line 16: The
   line 16: the
   line 18: the

3. a. line 7:   the city
      line 9:   The . . . part
      line 10: the river
      line 12: the . . . part
      line 16: The map
      line 16: the guidebook

   b. line 18: the information

   c. line 10: the . . . buildings

Exercise 2 (p. 64)

A. 2. The movies were interesting.
   3. X
   4. Houses are expensive.
   5. I saw tourists in the cities.
   6. X

B. 2. It's easy to find a good restaurant.
   3. Stay home on a rainy day.
   4. I ate an egg for breakfast.
   5. We often take a taxi.
   6. Give me the suitcase.

Exercise 3 (p. 64)

2. b, c
3. a, b
4. a
5. b
6. b

Exercise 4 (p. 65)

2. The trip was great.
3. Do you want a glass of water?
4. I like video games.
5. Who is the letter from?
6. I went to a museum.

Exercise 5 (p. 65)

Conversation 1
2. a
3. the
4. The
5. the

Conversation 2
1. a
2. the
3. Ø
4. A
5. a
6. an

Conversation 3
1. Ø
2. a
3. a
4. the
5. the

Exercise 6 (p. 66)

I really love ~~an~~ *the* old buildings and ~~x~~ *the* wonderful markets.

Yesterday I bought ∧*a* beautiful leather jacket for ~~the~~ *a* great

price. I'm sorry we're only staying for ∧*a* week!

   Love,

   Mary

Exercise 7 (p. 66)

Answers will vary.

Chapter 15 Quantity Expressions

Exercise 1 (p. 67)

1. **Quantity Expressions**
   line 7:   some
   line 10: some
   line 11: many

   Nouns
   line 7:   chicken and fish
   line 10: fish
   line 12: vegetables

2. Singular nouns: chicken, fish, fish
   Plural nouns: vegetables

3. any meat

Exercise 2 (p. 68)

2. any
3. a lot of
4. a little
5. many
6. a few
7. some
8. a lot
9. many
10. some

Exercise 3 (p. 68)

Answers will vary. Some examples are:
2. a few
3. many
4. any
5. a little
6. no

Exercise 4 (p. 69)

2. much
3. a lot of
4. some, a few
5. a few
6. some
7. a lot of
8. much

Exercise 5 (p. 69)

Answers will vary. Some examples are:
2. any problems.
3. some popcorn.
4. many languages.

5. much money.
6. a lot of help.

Exercise 6 (p. 70)

2. f
3. a
4. e
5. c
6. b

Exercise 7 (p. 70)

Answers will vary.

Chapter 16 *There Is* and *There Are*

Exercise 1 (p. 71)

1. line 7:   There is
   line 12: There are
   line 17: There are
   line 22: There is
   line 28: There are not

   line 7:   subway
   line 13: companies
   line 17: ships
   line 22: cruise
   line 28: laws

2. line 7:   There is no subway.
   line 28: There are not many city laws. . . .

   They are different because the first example uses "no" to express the negative, and the second uses "not".

3. There is not a subway.

Exercise 2 (p. 72)

A. 2. There are some flowers in the garden.
   3. There is a little food in the refrigerator.
   4. There are rectangles in the painting.

B. 2. There are no flowers in the garden. There aren't any flowers in the garden.
   3. There is no food in the refrigerator. There isn't any food in the refrigerator.
   4. There are no rectangles in the painting. There aren't any rectangles in the painting.

Exercise 3 (p. 72)

2. How many books are there in the library?
3. Is there an easy solution to the problem?
4. How much sugar is there in this dessert?
5. Is there much traffic in the afternoon?
6. Are there any good restaurants in the neighborhood?

Exercise 4 (p. 73)

2. There is no fountain.
3. There is a jogger.
4. There are six flowers.
5. There are no trees. OR There aren't any trees.
6. There is a gardener.
7. There are four dogs.
8. There are no snakes. OR There aren't any snakes.

Exercise 5 (p. 73)

2. A: Is there a leap year every three years?
   B: No, there isn't. There is a leap year every four years.
3. A: Are there ten dimes in a dollar?
   B: Yes, there are.
4. A: Are there 55 minutes in an hour?
   B: No, there aren't. There are 60 minutes in an hour.
5. A: Is there a full moon every month?
   B: Yes, there is.
6. A: Are there 54 weeks in a year?
   B: No, there aren't. There are 52 weeks in a year.

Exercise 6 (p. 74)

There *is* a subway system, but the subway lines only go through part of the city. There are many bus ~~line~~ *lines*. But the buses are often crowded. There ~~was~~ *were* streetcars in the past, but there ~~no~~ are *not* any streetcars now.

Most people in my city prefer to travel by car. People drive on the city streets or drive on the freeways. There is *a* very large freeway system. The freeways go almost everywhere in the city. But the freeways aren't always convenient because there is a lot of traffic.

Exercise 7 (p. 74)

Answers will vary.

See page 144 for Key to Review: Chapters 14–16.

Chapter 17 The Future with *Be Going To*

Exercise 1 (p. 77)

1. line 5:   're going to enjoy
   line 10: 'm going to fly
   line 18: are going to be
   line 21: 's going to do

2. line 20: 's not going to watch

3. *wh-* word + be + subject + *going to* + base form of verb
   What are you going to do Supergame Weekend?

Exercise 2 (p. 78)

2. The Lions are going to play the Bears.
3. The Lions aren't going to win the championship.
4. I'm going to buy my tickets online.
5. Our friends aren't going to go to the game with us.
6. They're going to meet us before the game.
7. We're going to take food for a picnic.
8. We're not going to be home late.

Exercise 3 (p. 78)

2. Are you going to go to the baseball game tomorrow?
3. Who is going to come for dinner on Thursday?
4. Is it going to rain this weekend?
5. How are you going to get to the airport?
6. Who is going to join the Red Sox next year?

Exercise 4 (p. 79)

Answers will vary. Some examples are:
2. am going to travel to Spain.
3. am going to study for the final exam.
4. are going to go to Vermont.
5. am going to graduate from college.
6. am going to read a good book.

Exercise 5 (p. 79)

Answers will vary. Some examples are:
2. He's not going to see the rock. He's going to fall.
3. He's going to score a goal. The goalie is not going to catch the ball.
4. The dog is not going to catch the cat. The cat is going to climb the tree.

Exercise 6 (p. 80)

Is Karen going to come, too? ~~You are~~ *Are you* going to bring food, or should we buy something there? And what *are* you going to do after the game? Do you want to come to our house?

In your opinion, who ~~be~~ *is* going to win this year? I don't have any idea, but I know it's going to ~~being~~ *to be* an exciting game. The Hurricanes really want to be champions this year. They ~~is~~ *are* going to play their best.

See you soon,

George

Exercise 7 (p. 80)

Answers will vary.

Chapter 18 The Future with *Will*

Exercise 1 (p. 81)

1. line 5: will work
   line 11: 'll leave
   line 12: 'll be
   line 13: 'll be
   line 13: 'll see

   The form of *will* does not change with different subjects.

2. line 10: won't be
   line 13: won't be

Exercise 2 (p. 82)

2. will
3. won't, will
4. won't, will
5. Will, will
6. will, will

Exercise 3 (p. 82)

Answers will vary. Some examples are:
2. They will save a lot of money. They won't buy a house for a long time.
3. She will apply for a new job. She won't stay at her present job for very long.
4. Victor will borrow a computer from a friend. He won't buy a new one.

Exercise 4 (p. 83)

2. I'll water the plants this afternoon.
3. I won't tell anyone.
4. I'll do the dishes in the morning.
5. I'll write it tomorrow.
6. I won't stay up late tonight.

Exercise 5 (p. 83)

Answers will vary. Some examples are:
2. I'll turn it off.
3. I'll take the black one.
4. I'll buy her a present.
5. I'll close the window.
6. I'll take the 6:30 flight.

Exercise 6 (p. 84)

2. b
3. a
4. a
5. b
6. c

Exercise 7 (p. 84)

Answers will vary.

See page 144 for Key to Review: Chapters 17–18.

Chapter 19 *May* and *Might* for Present and Future Possibility

Exercise 1 (p. 87)

1. line 8: may not
   line 10: might

   line 8: have
   line 10: work

2. No. *May* and *might* have the same form with different subjects.

3. The base form of the verb.

Exercise 2 (p. 88)

A. 2. I may be late tonight.
   3. Jean may not be happy about the news.
   4. I may not pass the course.

B. 2. She might take a trip soon.
   3. We might not be home before 3:00.
   4. They might not get married.

Exercise 3 (p. 88)

Answers will vary. Some examples are:
   2. may / might
   3. may / may not / might / might not
   4. may / might

Exercise 4 (p. 89)

   2. c
   3. b
   4. c
   5. a
   6. b

Exercise 5 (p. 89)

Answers will vary. Some examples are:
   2. She may not go to the party.
   3. You may see Dan today.
   4. I will miss my train.
   5. She's going to order take-out food.

Exercise 6 (p. 90)

   2. b
   3. b
   4. b
   5. b
   6. a

Exercise 7 (p. 90)

Answers will vary.

Chapter 20 *Can* and *Could* for Present and Past Ability

Exercise 1 (p. 91)

1. line 12: could
   line 15: couldn't
   line 20: Could
   line 25: couldn't
   line 27: Can
   line 30: can

   line 13: play
   line 15: play
   line 20: read
   line 25: read
   line 28: play
   line 30: (play)

2. line 15: I couldn't play
   line 25: I couldn't read

3. line 27: Can you still play the piano and the cello?
   line 30: Yes, I can. . . .

Exercise 2 (p. 92)

   2. Could you understand the lecture last night?
   3. Teresa couldn't come to the party last Sunday.
   4. I couldn't finish the race last week.
   5. Hiro could speak three languages as a child.
   6. I couldn't finish the test in one hour yesterday.
   7. Could you climb this mountain ten years ago?
   8. Hannah could read very quickly at age six.

Exercise 3 (p. 92)

   2. can
   3. can't
   4. couldn't
   5. Could
   6. can't
   7. can
   8. couldn't

Exercise 4 (p. 93)

   2. couldn't
   3. could
   4. couldn't
   5. couldn't
   6. can
   7. can't
   8. can
   9. can
   10. can't

Exercise 5 (p. 93)

2. couldn't hear the telephone.
3. can/could go skiing.
4. couldn't pay attention to the teacher.
5. can buy some new toys.
6. can sing opera.
7. couldn't get to work on time.
8. can't do the laundry.

Exercise 6 (p. 94)

1. A: I could ~~to~~ play the piano and sing.

   B: Which you ⟨could⟩ do better?

   A: I could sing better.

2. A: Can you ~~speaking~~ *speak* French?

   B: No, I ~~cann't~~ *can't*. Can you?

   A: Yes, and I can ~~to~~ speak a little German, too.

3. A: You ⟨can⟩ cook?

   B: I can ~~to~~ cook a little.

   A: What kinds of things you ⟨can⟩ cook?

   B: Oh, I can make simple dishes like spaghetti.

Exercise 7 (p. 94)

Answers will vary.

Chapter 21 Modals of Request and Permission

Exercise 1 (p. 95)

1. line 5: will
   line 7: will
   line 7: could
   line 8: Would
   line 9: Would

   line 5: check
   line 7: be
   line 7: check
   line 8: do
   line 9: empty

2. you

Exercise 2 (p. 96)

2. may
3. won't
4. can't
5. will
6. cannot

Exercise 3 (p. 96)

Answers will vary. Some examples are:

2. Can I have a chocolate?
3. Would you please help me?
4. Will you please open the window?
5. Would you read my essay?
6. May I use the telephone?

Exercise 4 (p. 97)

2. f
3. a
4. g
5. h
6. c
7. b
8. d

Exercise 5 (p. 97)

Answers will vary. Some examples are:

1. b. Can I use your pen?
   c. Could I leave now?

2. a. Would you borrow some tea?
   b. Could you do the laundry?
   c. Will you leave now?

Exercise 6 (p. 98)

2. A: ~~May~~ *Can* you take care of my house this weekend?

   B: Sorry, I can't.

3. A: ~~Will~~ *May* I use your umbrella?

   B: Of course. Go right ahead.

4. A: Could you please help me with the trash?

   B: Sorry, I ~~wouldn't~~ *can't*. I'm busy right now.

5. A: May I go to my room?

   B: No, you ~~mayn't~~ *may not*. Finish your dinner first.

6. A: Would you get some food for dinner?

   B: Of course. ~~I'd~~ *I'll* get some after work.

Exercise 7 (p. 98)

Answers will vary.

Chapter 22 Modals of Advice, Necessity, and Prohibition

Exercise 1 (p. 99)

1. line 2: have to
   line 3: have to
   line 5: have to
   line 8: shouldn't
   line 9: must
   line 10: don't have to
   line 10: don't have to

   line 2: take out
   line 3: clean
   line 5: be
   line 8: stay out
   line 9: be
   line 10: clean
   line 11: be

2. The base form of the verb.

3. The modals *must* and *should* don't change in form. The modal *have to* changes in form.

Exercise 2 (p. 100)

2. Holly doesn't have to study all night.
3. You shouldn't pay attention to her advice.
4. I don't have to take this class.
5. You must not come tonight.
6. We shouldn't call Rosa.

Exercise 3 (p. 100)

2. Should we buy a new car?
3. What time do you have to get up tomorrow?
4. Do I have to make a decision now?
5. What should I do now?

Exercise 4 (p. 101)

Answers will vary. Some examples are:
2. Brian shouldn't clean up after his roommate.
3. Doris should come to work on time.
4. They should find jobs and save money.
5. John shouldn't eat so much.
6. He should work late today.

Exercise 5 (p. 101)

Answers will vary. Some examples are:
2. You should go to bed soon.
3. We must pay this bill by the end of the month.
4. You must not smoke on an airplane.
5. You don't have to buy me a present.

Exercise 6 (p. 102)

2. That isn't polite. You must not ~~to~~ talk like that.

3. Tomorrow is a holiday, so you ~~haven't~~ *don't have* to go to bed early tonight.

4. Your room is a mess. You shouldn't ~~to~~ throw all your clothes on the floor.

5. You have ∧*to* come right home after school today.

6. You ~~has~~ *have* to get Tammy a present for her birthday.

Exercise 7 (p. 102)

Answers will vary.

See page 145 for Key to Review: Chapters 19–22.

Chapter 23 Object Pronouns; Direct and Indirect Objects

Exercise 1 (p. 105)

	LINE	DIRECT	INDIRECT
2. their families	4		✓
3. their houses	7	✓	
4. a large meal	11	✓	
5. their relatives	11		✓
6. small children	13		✓
7. red envelopes	13	✓	
8. relatives and friends	22	✓	

Exercise 2 (p. 106)

2. us
3. them
4. her
5. me
6. you
7. him
8. it

Exercise 3 (p. 106)

A. 2. My mother is preparing a special meal for my brother and me.
   3. Keiko explained the Japanese holiday to her American friends.
   4. Julie showed her new dress to Lee.
   5. Jack sent a card to Susie for her birthday.

B. 2. My mother is preparing a special meal for us.
   3. Keiko explained the Japanese holiday to them.
   4. Julie showed him her new dress.
   5. Jack sent her a card for her birthday.

Exercise 4 (p. 107)

Answers will vary. Some examples are:
2. to mothers
3. their teacher
4. loved ones
5. for the family
6. for their friends
7. to people
8. children

Exercise 5 (p. 107)

2. a
3. a
4. a
5. a OR b
6. a OR b
7. a
8. a OR b

Exercise 6 (p. 108)

2. b   3. b   4. a   5. b   6. a

Exercise 7 (p. 108)

Answers will vary.

Chapter 24 Infinitives and Gerunds After Verbs

Exercise 1 (p. 109)

1. line 4:   expected to do
   line 5:   needed to talk
   line 9:   decided to celebrate
   line 11: wanted to meet

2. line 7:   like celebrating
   line 9:   enjoyed walking
   line 10: liked seeing
   line 12: started working

Exercise 2 (p. 110)

2. taking
3. to help
4. to go
5. doing
6. to find
7. to see
8. making
9. walking
10. to return

Exercise 3 (p. 110)

2. I dislike taking long business trips.
3. Dave kept working on the project all week.
4. They enjoy playing the piano.
5. They need to give us a direct answer.
6. She plans to go shopping tomorrow.
7. I hope to finish this assignment tomorrow.
8. She avoided talking to me all day.

Exercise 4 (p. 111)

Answers will vary. Some examples are:
2. eating
3. to take
4. to rain/raining
5. watching/ to watch
6. to study
7. to buy
8. to take

Exercise 5 (p. 111)

2. Sue refuses to speak to George.
3. He keeps arriving late.
4. We discussed taking an art class.
5. I began to understand the lecture.
6. The secretary admitted to not locking the office.

Exercise 6 (p. 112)

2. a
3. b
4. a
5. b
6. b

Exercise 7 (p. 112)

Answers will vary.

See page 145 for Key to Review: Chapters 23–24.

Chapter 25 Comparatives

Exercise 1 (p. 115)

1. line 3:   taller
   line 3:   younger
   line 5:   more sociable
   line 6:   quieter
   line 8:   shorter
   line 9:   darker
   line 9:   more attractive
   line 11: prettier
   line 11: more outgoing

2. line 12: better

Exercise 2 (p. 116)

A.
2. ADV
3. ADJ
4. ADJ
5. ADJ
6. ADV
7. ADJ
8. ADJ
9. ADV
10. ADJ
11. ADJ
12. ADV

B.
2. more slowly
3. more interesting
4. better
5. friendlier/more friendly
6. more efficiently
7. slower
8. more useful
9. more cheaply
10. safer
11. more famous
12. better

Exercise 3 (p. 116)

2. healthier/more healthy
3. better
4. more accurately
5. cooler
6. more enjoyable
7. bigger
8. more responsibly
9. faster
10. heavier

Exercise 4 (p. 117)

Answers will vary. Some examples are:
2. George is a better student than Silvia. Silvia is a worse student than George.
3. George is older than Silvia. Silvia is younger than George.
4. Silvia talks faster than George. George talks more slowly than Silvia.
5. George is more intelligent than Silvia. Silvia is less intelligent than George.
6. Silvia dances better than George. George is a worse dancer than Silvia.

Exercise 5 (p. 117)

Answers will vary. Some examples are:
2. A giraffe is larger than a horse.
3. History is more interesting than mathematics.
4. Tennis is more enjoyable than golf.

Exercise 6 (p. 118)

Answers will vary. Some examples are:
2. Betty sings better than Susan. Susan sings worse than Betty.
3. The apples are cheaper than the pears. The pears are more expensive than the apples.
4. My old apartment was more convenient than my new apartment. My new apartment is less convenient than my old apartment.
5. I feel better today than yesterday. I felt worse yesterday than today.
6. Bob exercises more frequently than Dana. Dana exercises less frequently than Bob.

Exercise 7 (p. 118)

Answers will vary.

Chapter 26 Superlatives

Exercise 1 (p. 119)

1. line 8:   better
2. line 5:   most fluent
   line 9:   the most beautiful
   line 12: the best
   line 12: the worst
3. Adjectives: most fluent, the most beautiful, the worst
   Adverbs: the most fluently, the best

Exercise 2 (p. 120)

2. easy, easier, the easiest
3. good, better, the best
4. high, higher, the highest
5. bad, worse, the worst
6. expensive, more expensive, the most expensive
7. carefully, more carefully, the most carefully
8. small, smaller, the smallest
9. interesting, more interesting, the most interesting
10. slowly, more slowly, the slowest

Exercise 3 (p. 120)

2. the most efficiently
3. the most common
4. the best
5. the largest
6. the worst
7. the most fluently
8. the most comfortable
9. the most beautiful
10. the best

Exercise 4 (p. 121)

Answers will vary. Some examples are:

Conversation 1
 2. the best
 3. the most intelligent
 4. the hardest

Conversation 2
 1. cheaper
 2. the best

Exercise 5 (p. 121)

Answer will vary. Some examples are:
 2. The most beautiful movie actress is Julia Roberts.
 3. The best restaurant in my town is La Viola.
 4. The least expensive way to travel is by train.
 5. The most efficient way to learn a language is to speak it every day.

Exercise 6 (p. 122)

 2. Correct.

 3. My neighbors' apartment is very large. It's the
    largest apartment ~~than~~ *in* the building.

 4. Yuji drives the ~~most fastly~~ *fastest* of all my friends.

 5. Russian grammar is ~~the most~~ *more* difficult than Italian
    grammar.

 6. Correct.

 7. The Nile is the ~~longer~~ *longest* river in the world.

 8. Rick's a terrible tennis player. He plays the ~~baddest~~ *worst*
    of anyone I know.

Exercise 7 (p. 122)

Answers will vary.

See page 145 for Key to Review: Chapters 25–26.

Key to Chapter Reviews

Review: Chapters 1–3 (p. 13)

A.
1. am
2. 's
3. aren't / 're not
4. 's
5. isn't / 's not
6. Are
7. 'm
8. are

B.
9. It's warm. ~~Opens~~ *Open* the window.
10. Meet Dennis. He *'s* an employee here.
11. Where your mother is? *(Where is your mother?)*
12. We're students. ~~We no are~~ *We aren't/We're not* teachers.
13. Is interesting the book? *(Is the book interesting?)*
14. ~~I amn't~~ *I'm not* from Mexico.
15. ~~Not~~ *Don't* drive. Take a taxi.

C.
16. Don't make noise.
17. Add the milk.
18. Don't forget your assignment.
19. Come in, please. / Please come in.
20. Do not swallow.

D.
21. a
22. b
23. a
24. b
25. b

Review: Chapters 4–5 (p. 23)

A.
1. a country
2. an apartment
3. bracelet
4. Coffee
5. an employee
6. paper
7. a bag
8. Football
9. sugar
10. children

B.
11. a
12. a
13. b
14. b
15. a
16. b

C.
17. X
18. We're / We are engineers.
19. Please bring your book tomorrow.

20. It is / It's a beautiful city.
21. X
22. They aren't / are not expensive apartments.
23. The garages are large.
24. X
25. The woman isn't / is not a doctor.

Review: Chapters 6–7 (p. 33)

A.
1. Is today your birthday? / Is your birthday today?
2. What are John's brothers like?
3. How is the weather in your country?
4. Is Amy's car blue?
5. Whose book is on the table?
6. Where is my leather bag?
7. Are these pants OK?
8. Is Bob Diane's husband?

B.
9. 6
10. 5
11. 8
12. 3
13. 2
14. 7
15. 4
16. 1

C.
17. b
18. b
19. c
20. c
21. a
22. b
23. a
24. c
25. b

Review: Chapters 8–10 (p. 47)

A.
1. b
2. c
3. c
4. a
5. a
6. c
7. a
8. b
9. b
10. b

B.
11. Jackie almost never/rarely drinks milk.
12. Do you sometimes drive too fast? OR Do you ever drive too fast?
13. The bus hardly ever comes late. OR The bus doesn't generally come late.
14. Bob doesn't ever stay out after midnight.

C. 15. Does your brother ~~to~~ work?

16. Ana seldom ~~calling~~ *calls* me on the weekends.

17. I ~~eating~~ *eat* in the cafeteria every day.

18. The children ~~watch~~ *are watching* TV right now.

19. What *are* you doing these days?

20. Dan remembers (seldom) his wife's birthday.

21. Does Anita ~~gets~~ *get* good grades?

22. We are ~~save~~ *saving* lots of money. / We ~~are~~ save lots of money.

23. Alan doesn't ~~never~~ *ever* take the bus. / Alan ~~doesn't~~ never ~~take~~ *takes* the bus.

24. We ~~no~~ *don't* take a long vacation every year.

25. Lisa usually ~~study~~ *studies* in the library.

Review: Chapters 11–13 (p. 61)

A. 1. a
2. b
3. c
4. b
5. c
6. b
7. a
8. b
9. a
10. b

B. 11. e
12. f
13. a
14. b
15. d
16. c

C. 17. I *was* born in 1979.

18. Sara *did* not ~~enjoyed~~ *enjoy* the play.

19. Why ~~wasn't~~ *didn't* you call me last night?

20. I ~~no~~ *did not* finish my homework last night.

21. Who ~~did send~~ *sent* the letter?

22. When *did* you ~~woke~~ *wake* up this morning?

23. I was cleaning house while you *were* resting.

24. Bill and I ~~was~~ *were* good friends in high school.

25. ~~Was~~ *Did* John win the prize yesterday?

Review: Chapters 14–16 (p. 75)

A. 1. a
2. b
3. c
4. c
5. b
6. a
7. a
8. a

B. 9. How ~~many~~ *much* traffic is there in your town?

10. There are ~~much~~ *many* people in the park.

11. Hurry up. The movie is starting in a ~~little~~ *few* minutes.

12. Small towns don't usually have ~~a~~ department stores. OR Small towns don't usually have a department ~~stores~~ *store*.

13. It's a good idea to get *a* map in a new city.

14. The neighborhood doesn't have a lot *of* restaurants.

C. 15. the
16. much
17. a little
18. a
19. How much
20. Is there
21. There is
22. a lot of
23. There are
24. some
25. How many

Review: Chapters 17–18 (p. 85)

A. 1. b
2. c
3. a
4. c
5. b
6. b
7. c
8. b

B. 9. What are you going *to* do this afternoon?

10. Joe ~~willn't~~ *won't* take a biology class.

11. The Tigers *are* not going to win the championship.

12. When are you going to ~~starting~~ *start* your new job?

13. I *am* not going to be in class tomorrow.

14. We'll ~~to~~ see you on Saturday.

15. What time ~~we are~~ [go] going to have lunch?

16. Carol will ~~goes~~ [go] to bed early tonight.

17. They are ~~going not~~ [not going] to drive to Chicago.

C. 18. b
19. c
20. c
21. b
22. b
23. c
24. c
25. a

Review: Chapters 19–22 (p. 103)

A. 1. May I borrow your math book?
2. Will I see you at the picnic this weekend?
3. Can I help you?
4. Would you drive me to school?
5. Does she have to work late tonight?
6. When should we take our vacation this year?
7. When could I see you?
8. Do you have to get up early tomorrow?

B. 9. 2
10. 4
11. 6
12. 1
13. 5
14. 8
15. 7
16. 3

C. 17. b
18. c
19. a
20. a
21. c
22. a
23. b
24. b
25. a

Review: Chapters 23–24 (p. 113)

A. 1. a, b
2. b
3. b, c
4. a
5. c
6. a, b
7. b
8. b, c

B. 9. Can you explain ~~us~~ the problem [to us]?

10. I dislike ~~to do~~ [doing] the laundry.

11. When you get home, please ~~me write~~ [write me] a letter.

12. Kate is finally learning ~~speaking~~ [to speak] Spanish.

13. Do you enjoy ~~to play~~ [playing] volleyball?

14. Did she show ~~you it~~ [it to you]?

15. George sent a postcard [to] me.

C. 16. b
17. a
18. c
19. c
20. b
21. c
22. b
23. a
24. c
25. b

Review: Chapters 25–26 (p. 123)

A. 1. oldest
2. younger
3. older
4. the best
5. the most popular
6. harder
7. larger
8. smaller
9. prettier
10. the most beautiful

B. 11. Yesterday was ~~more hot~~ [hotter] than today.

12. I think Mexican food is ~~a~~ [the] most delicious.

13. Is Chinese harder to learn ~~from~~ [than] German?

14. Janice is the ~~better~~ [best] writer in the class.

15. Dana runs ~~the~~ faster than Mike.

16. There are ~~few~~ [fewer] monolingual people in Denmark than in England.

17. Who is the ~~baddest~~ [worst] player on the team?

18. Kim speaks the ~~most~~ slowest.

19. A kilo weighs ~~the~~ more than a pound.

C. 20. c
21. b
22. a
23. a
24. b
25. c